hymnal  supplement 98

Prepared by The Commission on Worship of
The Lutheran Church—Missouri Synod

HYMNAL SUPPLEMENT 98
PEW EDITION

Also Available:
    Accompaniment Edition (97-6752)
    Daily Prayer Cards (10-pack) (S14969)
    Large Print and Braille editions
    Vocal Descants Edition (97-6718)
    Instrumental Descants Edition (97-6719)
    Handbell Descants Edition (97-6720)
    Hymnal Supplement 98 Handbook (S14943)

Cover artwork: Luther seal courtesy of Concordia Seminary, St. Louis

Scripture quotations are from the HOLY BIBLE: NEW INTERNATIONAL VERSION,
© 1973, 1978, 1984 by International Bible Society. Used by permission of Zondervan
Publishing House. All rights reserved.

The Scripture quotations in this book marked NKJV are from New King James
edition, copyright © 1979, 1982. Used by permission.

Luther's Small Catechism © 1986 Concordia Publishing House.

ISBN 0-570-01212-0

Copyright © 1998 Concordia Publishing House
3558 S. Jefferson Avenue, St. Louis, MO 63118-3968
Manufactured in the United States of America

3 4 5 6 7 8 9 10   07 06 05 04 03 02 01 00 99

CONTENTS

INTRODUCTION

"The Lord Almighty order our days and our deeds in His peace."

The gifts of God come to us in many and various ways, but never so certainly as in the Divine Service of the Church. Here God delivers forgiveness, life, and salvation through His Word and holy sacraments, which are the means of His grace.

Here also God orders "our days and our deeds" as He did in creation. That order is still present in our daily lives as a gift. Luther spoke of that order when he listed "discipline" as one of the gifts of daily bread. We are blessed with such order in the liturgy and hymns of the Church. They guide the Church's worship in the Word and sacraments. They give the Church a common language, as Luther encouraged in the Preface to the Small Catechism. Together with Bible and catechism, the hymnal has always been a blessed treasury for the formation of the people's piety.

A hymnal is more than hymns, for through liturgy, psalmody, and hymnody, the Church is gathered into the very presence of the living Christ. Either with direct quotation or paraphrase, we are given to speak the words and to sing the songs of Scripture itself.

A hymnal is more than a congregational resource, since it serves the whole life of prayer. With it families, small groups, and individuals are led into the riches of God's Word. Thus it is also a book for instruction in the faith—in a word, catechesis.

A hymnal serves more than today's generation, for it serves timelessly the needs of the Church in every age. Furthermore, it offers more than we sometimes want or like because it gives voice to God's message and to our response for what we need.

Hymnal Supplement 98 is intended to serve the Church with additional resources for worship. Intentionally a supplement, it is not a replacement for the hymnal. It is intended specifically to offer simplified forms of congregational services as well as forms for family and group devotions. This supplement provides for special services of the Church, such as midweek Advent and Lenten services. Intended to be devotional yet churchly, it serves the needs of God's people within the context of the whole Church.

Gathering hymns from a wide range of time, place, and Christian community, this supplement is a catholic collection. It recovers the use of some Bach chorales while expanding the repertoire to hymnody of Africa, China, and Latin America. It includes some of the earliest texts of the Church while adding the voices of 20th-century authors and composers.

The following are features of this supplement:
- Scripture references are included for most hymns and portions of the liturgy.
- Rubrics and options have been kept to a minimum in the liturgies.
- Liturgical materials have been designed not only for ease of use but also for understanding the basic structure of the services.
- The psalms, while modest in number, have been selected to give voice to every season of the church year.

It is the prayer of the Commission on Worship that *Hymnal Supplement 98* will be an instrument of service to the Church, that with it the Gospel be honored, God's people be taught, and the Church's pastors be guided. This supplement is intended to serve God's people that, in the words of Nikolaus Selnecker, the Church might be "strong, bold, unified in act and song."

DIVINE SERVICE

PREPARATION

Stand

INVOCATION

The sign of the cross may be made by all in remembrance of their Baptism.

P In the name of the Father and of the ✠ Son and of the Holy Spirit.

C **Amen.**

Kneel/Stand

CONFESSION

P If You, O Lord, kept a record of sins,

C **O Lord, who could stand?**

P But with You there is forgiveness;

C **therefore You are feared.** *Psalm 130:3–4*

Silence for reflection on God's Word and for self-examination.

P O almighty God, merciful Father,

C **I, a poor, miserable sinner, confess to You all my sins and iniquities with which I have ever offended You and justly deserved Your punishment now and forever. But I am heartily sorry for them and sincerely repent of them, and I pray You of Your boundless mercy and for the sake of the holy, innocent, bitter sufferings and death of Your beloved Son, Jesus Christ, to be gracious and merciful to me, a poor sinful being.**

ABSOLUTION

The minister stands and pronounces the ABSOLUTION.

P Upon this your confession, I, by virtue of my office as a called and ordained servant of the Word, announce the grace of God to all of you, and in the stead and by the command of my Lord Jesus Christ I forgive you all your sins in the name of the Father and of the ✠ Son and of the Holy Spirit.

C **Amen.**

Stand

SERVICE OF THE WORD

ENTRANCE HYMN or Introit or Psalm

KYRIE
Mark 10:47

Lord, have mer - cy on us; Christ, have mer - cy on us; Lord, have mer - cy on us.

GLORIA IN EXCELSIS
Luke 2:14

During Advent and Lent the GLORIA IN EXCELSIS is omitted.

1 Glo - ry to God, we give You thanks and praise;
2 Lord Je - sus Christ, the Fa - ther's on - ly Son,
3 A - lone, O Christ, You on - ly are the Lord,

Of heav'n - ly joy and earth - ly peace we sing.
You bore for us the load of this world's sin.
At God's right hand in maj - es - ty most high:

We wor - ship You, to You our hearts we raise,
O Lamb of God, Your glo - rious vic - t'ry won,
Who, with the Spir - it wor - shiped and a - dored,

Lord God, al - might - y Fa - ther, heav'n - ly King.
Re - ceive our prayer, grant us Your peace with - in.
With all the heav'n - ly host we glo - ri - fy.

7

SALUTATION AND COLLECT OF THE DAY

P The Lord be with you.

C And with your spirit.

P Let us pray. . . .

C Amen.

Sit

OLD TESTAMENT READING

After the reading:

A This is the Word of the Lord.

C Thanks be to God.

PSALM or Gradual

EPISTLE

After the reading:

A This is the Word of the Lord.

C Thanks be to God.

Stand

GOSPEL ACCLAMATION

During Lent the GOSPEL ACCLAMATION is omitted.

C Al - le - lu - ia. Al - le - lu - ia. Al - le - lu - ia.

The congregation sings the following, or the choir may sing an appointed verse:

C These things are writ - ten that you may be - lieve that

Je - sus is the Christ, the Son of God.

John 20:31

C Al - le - lu - ia. Al - le - lu - ia. Al - le - lu - ia.

HOLY GOSPEL

Ⓟ The Holy Gospel according to St. _____, the _____ chapter.

Ⓒ **Glory to You, O Lord.**

After the reading:

Ⓟ This is the Gospel of the Lord.

Ⓒ **Praise to You, O Christ.**

NICENE CREED

Ⓒ **I believe in one God,**
    the Father Almighty,
    maker of heaven and earth
        and of all things visible and invisible.

  And in one Lord Jesus Christ,
    the only-begotten Son of God,
    begotten of His Father before all worlds,
    God of God, Light of Light,
    very God of very God,
    begotten, not made,
    being of one substance with the Father,
    by whom all things were made;
    who for us men and for our salvation
        came down from heaven
    and was incarnate by the Holy Spirit of the virgin Mary
    and was made man;
    and was crucified also for us under Pontius Pilate.
    He suffered and was buried.
    And the third day He rose again
        according to the Scriptures
        and ascended into heaven
    and sits at the right hand of the Father.
    And He will come again with glory to judge
        both the living and the dead,
    whose kingdom will have no end.

  And I believe in the Holy Spirit,
    the Lord and giver of life,
    who proceeds from the Father and the Son,
    who with the Father and the Son together
        is worshiped and glorified,
    who spoke by the prophets.
    And I believe in one holy Christian and apostolic Church,*
    I acknowledge one Baptism for the remission of sins,
    and I look for the resurrection of the dead
    and the life ✠ of the world to come. Amen.

*The ancient text: one holy catholic and apostolic Church

Sit

HYMN OF THE DAY

SERMON

Stand/Kneel

PRAYER OF THE CHURCH

Ⓐ Let us pray for the whole people of God in Christ Jesus and for all people according to their needs.

After each portion of the prayer:

Ⓐ Lord, in Your mercy,
Ⓒ **hear our prayer.**

Ⓐ Let us pray to the Lord.
Ⓒ **Lord, have mercy.**

The prayer concludes:

Ⓟ Into Your hands, O Lord, we commend all for whom we pray, trusting in Your mercy; through Your Son, Jesus Christ, our Lord.
Ⓒ **Amen.**

Sit

OFFERING

SERVICE OF THE SACRAMENT

Stand

PREFACE

Ⓟ The Lord be with you.
Ⓒ **And with your spirit.**

Ⓟ Lift up your hearts.
Ⓒ **We lift them to the Lord.**

Ⓟ Let us give thanks to the Lord our God.
Ⓒ **It is right to give Him thanks and praise.**

The preface appropriate to the day or season is said.

P It is truly good, right, and salutary . . . evermore praising You and saying:

SANCTUS

Isaiah 6:3; Matthew 21:9

Ho-ly, ho-ly, ho-ly Lord, God of Sa-ba-oth, a-dored; Heav'n and earth with full ac-claim shout the glo-ry of Your name. Sing ho-san-na in the high-est, sing ho-san-na to the Lord; Tru-ly blest is He who comes in the name of the Lord!

PRAYER OF THANKSGIVING

P Blessed are You, O Lord our God, king of all creation, for You have had mercy on us and given Your only-begotten Son that whoever believes in Him should not perish but have eternal life.

The prayer continues with the following, or a prayer appropriate to the season is said.

In Your righteous judgment You condemned the sin of Adam and Eve, who ate the forbidden fruit, and You justly barred them and all their children from the tree of life. Yet, in Your great mercy, You promised salvation by a second Adam, Your Son, Jesus Christ, our Lord, and made His cross a life-giving tree for all who trust in Him.

We give You thanks for the redemption You have prepared for us through Jesus Christ. Grant us Your Holy Spirit that we may faithfully eat and drink of the fruits of His cross and receive the blessings of forgiveness, life, and salvation that come to us in His body and blood.

The prayer concludes:

Hear us as we pray in His name and as He has taught us:

C Our Father who art in heaven,
   hallowed be Thy name,
   Thy kingdom come,
   Thy will be done
      on earth as it is in heaven.
   Give us this day our daily bread;
   and forgive us our trespasses
      as we forgive those
      who trespass against us;
   and lead us not into temptation,
      but deliver us from evil.
   For Thine is the kingdom
      and the power and the glory
      forever and ever. Amen.

C Our Father in heaven,
   hallowed be Your name,
   Your kingdom come,
   Your will be done
      on earth as in heaven.
   Give us today our daily bread.
   Forgive us our sins
      as we forgive those
      who sin against us.
   Lead us not into temptation,
      but deliver us from evil.
   For the kingdom, the power,
      and the glory are Yours
      now and forever. Amen.

Matthew 6:9–13

WORDS OF INSTITUTION

P Our Lord Jesus Christ, on the night when He was betrayed, took bread, and when He had given thanks, He broke it and gave it to the disciples and said: Take, eat; this is My ✠ body, which is given for you. This do in remembrance of Me.

In the same way also He took the cup after supper, and when He had given thanks, He gave it to them, saying: Drink of it, all of you; this is My ✠ blood of the new testament, which is shed for you for the forgiveness of sins. This do, as often as you drink it, in remembrance of Me.

PEACE OF THE LORD

P The peace of the Lord be with you always.

C Amen.

AGNUS DEI

John 1:29

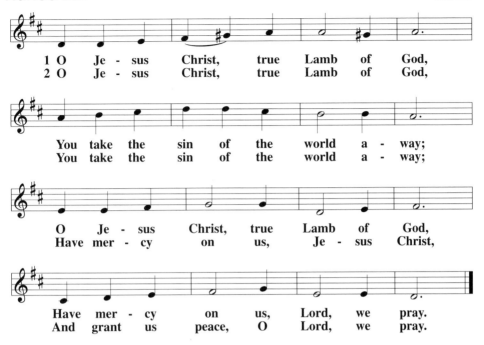

1 O Je - sus Christ, true Lamb of God,
2 O Je - sus Christ, true Lamb of God,

You take the sin of the world a - way;
You take the sin of the world a - way;

O Je - sus Christ, true Lamb of God,
Have mer - cy on us, Je - sus Christ,

Have mer - cy on us, Lord, we pray.
And grant us peace, O Lord, we pray.

Sit

DISTRIBUTION

The minister and those who assist him receive the body and blood of Christ first and then distribute them to those who come to receive, saying:

Take, eat; this is the true body of our Lord and Savior Jesus Christ, given into death for your sins.

Take, drink; this is the true blood of our Lord and Savior Jesus Christ, shed for the forgiveness of your sins.

The very body of Christ, given for you.

The very blood of Christ, shed for you.

In dismissing the communicants, the following is said:

℗ The body and blood of our Lord strengthen and preserve you steadfast in the true faith to life everlasting. Go in peace.

⬛ **Amen.**

Stand

NUNC DIMITTIS

Luke 2:29–32

1 O Lord, now let Your ser - vant De -
2 All glo - ry to the Fa - ther, All

part in heav'n - ly peace, For I have seen the
glo - ry to the Son, All glo - ry to the

glo - ry Of Your re - deem - ing grace: A
Spir - it, For - ev - er Three - in - One; For

light to lead the Gen - tiles Un -
as in the be - gin - ning, Is

to Your ho - ly hill, The glo - ry of Your
now, shall ev - er be, God's tri - une name re -

peo - ple, Your cho - sen Is - ra - el.
sound - ing Through all e - ter - ni - ty.

POST-COMMUNION COLLECT

Ⓐ Let us pray.

Ⓐ We give thanks to You, almighty God, that You have refreshed us through this salutary gift, and we implore You that of Your mercy You would strengthen us through the same in faith toward You and in fervent love toward one another; through Jesus Christ, Your Son, our Lord, who lives and reigns with You and the Holy Spirit, one God, now and forever.

Ⓐ O God the Father, the fountain and source of all goodness, who in loving-kindness sent Your only-begotten Son into the flesh, we thank You that for His sake You have given us pardon and peace in this sacrament, and we ask You not to forsake Your children but always to rule our hearts and minds by Your Holy Spirit that we may be enabled to serve You constantly; through Jesus Christ, Your Son, our Lord, who lives and reigns with You and the Holy Spirit, one God, now and forever.

Ⓐ Gracious God, our heavenly Father, You have given us a foretaste of the feast to come in the Holy Supper of Your Son's body and blood. Keep us firm in the true faith throughout our days of pilgrimage that, on the Day of His coming, we may, together with all Your saints, celebrate the marriage feast of the Lamb in His kingdom, which has no end; through Jesus Christ, Your Son, our Lord, who lives and reigns with You and the Holy Spirit, one God, now and forever.

Ⓒ **Amen.**

BENEDICAMUS AND BENEDICTION

Ⓐ Let us bless the Lord.

Ⓒ **Thanks be to God.**

Ⓟ The Lord bless you and keep you.
The Lord make His face shine on you and be gracious to you.
The Lord lift up His countenance on you and ✠ give you peace.

Numbers 6:24–26

Ⓒ **Amen.**

Notes on the Liturgy

1. PREPARATION—The CONFESSION and ABSOLUTION may be omitted.

2. KYRIE—During Lent, one of the following settings of the KYRIE may be substituted:
   • Hymn 913, "Kyrie"
   • Hymn 820, "Your Heart, O God"

3. GLORIA IN EXCELSIS—In order to avoid a cluttered page, additional biblical references are provided here:

   John 1:29; Ephesians 1:20–21; Revelation 7:9–12.

   During the Sundays of Easter, the following settings of "Worthy Is Christ" *(Dignus es)* may be used in place of the GLORIA:
   • Hymn 896, "Alabaré"
   • Hymn 910, "Splendor and Honor"

4. OLD TESTAMENT READING—During the Sundays of Easter the three-year lectionary provides a reading from Acts.

5. GOSPEL ACCLAMATION—Hymn 907, "Alleluia" may be used as an alternate.

6. PRAYER OF THE CHURCH—Prayers may be included for the whole Church, the nations, those in need, the parish, special concerns, etc.

7. OFFERING—A hymn appropriate to the season may be sung.

8. NUNC DIMITTIS—An alternate setting (Hymn 911, "Lord, Bid Your Servant") or an appropriate hymn may be substituted.

EVENING PRAYER

Stand

SERVICE OF LIGHT

GENERAL

L. Jesus Christ is the Light of the world,

C. **the light no darkness can overcome.**

L. Stay with us, Lord, for it is evening,

C. **and the day is almost over.**

L. Let Your light scatter the darkness

C. **and illumine Your Church.**

ADVENT

L. The Spirit and the Church cry out:

C. **Come, Lord Jesus.**

L. All those who await His appearance pray:

C. **Come, Lord Jesus.**

L. The whole creation pleads:

C. **Come, Lord Jesus.**

LENT

L. Now is the time of God's favor;

C. **now is the day of salvation.**

L. Turn us again, O God of our salvation,

C. **that the light of Your face may shine on us.**

L. May Your justice shine like the sun;

C. **and may the poor be lifted up.**

As the hymn is sung, the candles on and near the altar are lighted.

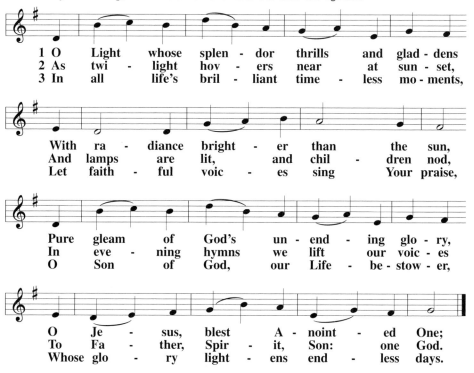

1 O Light whose splen - dor thrills and glad - dens
2 As twi - light hov - ers near at sun - set,
3 In all life's bril - liant time - less mo - ments,

With ra - diance bright - er than the sun,
And lamps are lit, and chil - dren nod,
Let faith - ful voic - es sing Your praise,

Pure gleam of God's un - end - ing glo - ry,
In eve - ning hymns we lift our voic - es
O Son of God, our Life - be - stow - er,

O Je - sus, blest A - noint - ed One;
To Fa - ther, Spir - it, Son: one God.
Whose glo - ry light - ens end - less days.

Ⓛ Let us give thanks to the Lord our God.

Ⓒ **It is right to give Him thanks and praise.**

Ⓛ Blessed are You, O Lord our God, king of the universe, who led Your people Israel by a pillar of cloud by day and a pillar of fire by night. Enlighten our darkness by the light of Your Christ; may His Word be a lamp to our feet and a light to our path; for You are merciful, and You love Your whole creation and we, Your creatures, glorify You, Father, Son, and Holy Spirit.

Ⓒ **Amen.**

Sit

PSALM

HYMN

READINGS

One or two readings follow. After each reading:

Ⓛ This is the Word of the Lord.

Ⓒ **Thanks be to God.**

Silence for reflection on God's Word may follow each reading.

18

At the conclusion of the readings, the following is said:

Ⓛ In many and various ways God spoke to His people of old by the prophets.

Ⓒ **But now in these last days He has spoken to us by His Son.**   *Hebrews 1:1–2*

Stand

MAGNIFICAT
Luke 1:46–55

1 My soul re - joic - es, My spir - it voic - es— Sing the
2 His arm now bar - ing, His strength de - clar - ing—Sing the

great-ness of the Lord! For God my Sav - ior Has shown me
great-ness of the Lord! The proud He scat - ters, Their rule He

fa - vor—Sing the great - ness of the Lord! With praise and
shat - ters—Sing the great - ness of the Lord! Op - pres - sion

bless - ing, Join in con - fess - ing God, who is
hal - ted; The meek ex - alt - ed. Full are the

sole - ly Might - y and ho - ly— Oh, sing the
hun - gry; Emp - ty, the wealth - y— Oh, sing the

great - ness of God the Lord! His ten - der mer - cy Shall rest se -
great - ness of God the Lord! Here is the to - ken All that was

cure - ly On all who fear Him, Love and re -
spo - ken To A - br'am's off - spring God is ful -

vere Him—Oh, sing the great - ness of God the Lord!
fill - ing— Oh, sing the great - ness of God the Lord!

Kneel/Stand

LITANY

The LITANY may be said, or it may be sung according to the following musical form. The congregation's response should begin as the petition sung by the leader ends so that the word "Lord" is sung simultaneously by both.

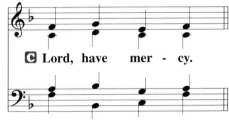

Ⓛ For the peace from above and for our salvation let us pray to the Lord.

Ⓒ **Lord, have mercy.**

Ⓛ For the peace of the whole world, for the well-being of the Church of God, and for the unity of all let us pray to the Lord.

Ⓒ **Lord, have mercy.**

Ⓛ For this holy house and for all who offer here their worship and praise let us pray to the Lord.

Ⓒ **Lord, have mercy.**

Ⓛ For _names_ , our *pastor/pastors* in Christ, for all servants of the Church, and for all the people, let us pray to the Lord.

Ⓒ **Lord, have mercy.**

Ⓛ For our public servants, for the government and those who protect us, that they may be upheld and strengthened in every good deed, let us pray to the Lord.

Ⓒ **Lord, have mercy.**

Ⓛ For those who work to bring peace, justice, health, and protection in this and every place let us pray to the Lord.

Ⓒ **Lord, have mercy.**

Ⓛ For those who bring offerings, those who do good works in this congregation, those who toil, those who sing, and all the people here present who await from the Lord great and abundant mercy let us pray to the Lord.

Ⓒ **Lord, have mercy.**

Ⓛ For favorable weather, for an abundance of the fruits of the earth, and for peaceful times let us pray to the Lord.

Ⓒ **Lord, have mercy.**

Ⓛ For our deliverance from all affliction, wrath, danger, and need let us pray to the Lord.

Ⓒ **Lord, have mercy.**

Ⓛ For the faithful who have gone before us and are with Christ let us give thanks to the Lord.

Ⓒ **Alleluia.** (*during Lent:* **Thanks be to God.**)

Ⓛ Help, save, comfort, and defend us, gracious Lord.

Silence for meditation.

Ⓛ Rejoicing in the fellowship of all the saints, let us commend ourselves, one another, and our whole life to Christ, our Lord.

Ⓒ **To You, O Lord.**

Ⓛ O God, from whom come all holy desires, all good counsels, and all just works, give to us, Your servants, that peace which the world cannot give, that our hearts may be set to obey Your commandments; and also that we, being defended from the fear of our enemies, may live in peace and quietness; through the merits of Jesus Christ, our Savior, who lives and reigns with You and the Holy Spirit, God forever.

Ⓒ **Amen.**

Ⓛ Lord, remember us in Your kingdom, and teach us to pray:

Ⓒ **Our Father who art in heaven,**
　　hallowed be Thy name,
　　Thy kingdom come,
　　Thy will be done
　　　　on earth as it is in heaven.
Give us this day our daily bread;
and forgive us our trespasses
　　as we forgive those
　　who trespass against us;
and lead us not into temptation,
　　but deliver us from evil.
For Thine is the kingdom
　　and the power and the glory
　　forever and ever. Amen.

Ⓒ **Our Father in heaven,**
　　hallowed be Your name,
　　Your kingdom come,
　　Your will be done
　　　　on earth as in heaven.
Give us today our daily bread.
Forgive us our sins
　　as we forgive those
　　who sin against us.
Lead us not into temptation,
　　but deliver us from evil.
For the kingdom, the power,
　　and the glory are Yours
　　now and forever. Amen.

Matthew 6:9–13

Stand

L Let us bless the Lord.

C Thanks be to God.

When there is no sermon, the service concludes with the Blessing.

OFFERING

HYMN

SERMON

Stand

PRAYER

One of the following prayers is said.

P Almighty God, grant to Your Church Your Holy Spirit and the wisdom which comes down from heaven that Your Word may not be bound but have free course and be preached to the joy and edifying of Christ's holy people, that in steadfast faith we may serve You and in the confession of Your name may abide to the end; through Jesus Christ, our Lord.

P Lord God, You have called Your servants to ventures of which we cannot see the ending, by paths as yet untrodden, through perils unknown. Give us faith to go out with good courage, not knowing where we go but only that Your hand is leading us and Your love supporting us; through Jesus Christ, our Lord.

P Lord, we thank You that You have taught us what You would have us believe and do. Help us by Your Holy Spirit, for the sake of Jesus Christ, to hold fast Your Word in hearts which You have cleansed that thereby we may be made strong in faith and perfect in holiness, and be comforted in life and in death.

C Amen.

BLESSING

P The almighty and merciful Lord, the Father, the ✠ Son, and the Holy Spirit, bless and preserve you.

L The almighty and merciful Lord, the Father, the ✠ Son, and the Holy Spirit, bless and preserve us.

C Amen.

Notes on the Liturgy

1. The service may begin with a procession in which a large, lighted candle is carried to its stand in front of the congregation.

2. Additional seasonal sentences for the SERVICE OF LIGHT may be found in *Lutheran Worship,* pp. 288–90.

3. In order to avoid a cluttered page, the biblical references for the opening sentences on page 17 are provided here. The brackets indicate verses that are reflected, though not directly quoted, in the sentences.

   General: [John 8:12; 1:5]; Luke 24:49; [1 Corinthians 4:5; 2 Corinthians 4:6]

   Advent: [Revelation 22:17; Galatians 4:6; Titus 2:13; 2 Timothy 4:8; Romans 8:22]

   Lent: 2 Corinthians 6:2; Isaiah 49:8; [Psalm 85:4] Psalm 4:6; [Numbers 6:25; Amos 5:24; 1 Samuel 2:8]

   Biblical references for the hymn on page 18 are Matthew 3:16–17; John 1:4–5; 12:46; Colossians 1:15.

4. More than one PSALM may be sung or said; Psalm 141 may be used first.

5. An alternate setting of the MAGNIFICAT (Hymn 909) may be substituted. Settings of the NUNC DIMITTIS (page 14 and Hymn 911) may also be substituted.

RESPONSIVE PRAYER

OPENING VERSICLES

L O Lord, open my lips,

C **and my mouth will declare Your praise.**   *Psalm 51:15*

L Make haste, O God, to deliver me;

C **make haste to help me, O Lord.**   *Psalm 70:1*

**Glory be to the Father and to the Son and to the Holy Spirit;
as it was in the beginning, is now, and will be forever. Amen.**

A psalm may be sung or said.

READING(S)

After the reading(s):

L This is the Word of the Lord.

C **Thanks be to God.**

A hymn or canticle may be sung or said.

PRAYERS

L Lord, have mercy.   *Mark 10:47*

C **Christ, have mercy.**

L Lord, have mercy.

C Our Father who art in heaven,
　　hallowed be Thy name,
　　Thy kingdom come,
　　Thy will be done
　　　on earth as it is in heaven.
Give us this day our daily bread;
and forgive us our trespasses
　　as we forgive those
　　who trespass against us;
and lead us not into temptation,
　　but deliver us from evil.
For Thine is the kingdom
　　and the power and the glory
　　forever and ever. Amen.

C Our Father in heaven,
　　hallowed be Your name,
　　Your kingdom come,
　　Your will be done
　　　on earth as in heaven.
Give us today our daily bread.
Forgive us our sins
　　as we forgive those
　　who sin against us.
Lead us not into temptation,
　　but deliver us from evil.
For the kingdom, the power,
　　and the glory are Yours
　　now and forever. Amen.

Matthew 6:9–13

C I believe in God, the Father Almighty,
　　maker of heaven and earth.

And in Jesus Christ, His only Son, our Lord,
　　who was conceived by the Holy Spirit,
　　born of the virgin Mary,
　　suffered under Pontius Pilate,
　　was crucified, died and was buried.
He descended into hell.
The third day He rose again from the dead.
He ascended into heaven
　　and sits at the right hand of God, the Father Almighty.
From thence He will come to judge the living and the dead.

I believe in the Holy Spirit,
　　the holy Christian Church,
　　the communion of saints,
　　the forgiveness of sins,
　　the resurrection of the body,
　　and the life ✠ everlasting. Amen.

L Hear my prayer, O Lord;

C listen to my cry for mercy.

L In the day of my trouble I will call to You,

C for You will answer me.

Psalm 86:6–7

25

L Hide Your face from my sins

C **and blot out all my iniquity.**

L Create in me a pure heart, O God,

C **and renew a steadfast spirit within me.**

L Do not cast me from Your presence

C **or take Your Holy Spirit from me.**

L Restore to me the joy of Your salvation

C **and grant me a willing spirit to sustain me.** *Psalm 51:9–12*

L Because Your loving kindness is better than life,

C **my lips shall praise You.**

L Because You have been my help,

C **therefore in the shadow of Your wings I will rejoice.** *Psalm 63:3,7 NKJV*

L Teach me Your way, O Lord, and I will walk in Your truth;

C **give me an undivided heart, that I may fear Your name.**

L I will praise You, O Lord, my God, with all my heart;

C **I will glorify Your name forever.** *Psalm 86:11–12*

L May all who seek You rejoice and be glad in You;

C **may those who love Your salvation always say,
"Let God be exalted."** *Psalm 70:4*

L Save Your people and bless Your inheritance;

C **be their shepherd and carry them forever.** *Psalm 28:9*

L Hear my prayer, O Lord;

C **listen to my cry for mercy.** *Psalm 86:6*

The COLLECT OF THE DAY and other suitable collects may be prayed. The prayers may conclude with Luther's Morning or Evening Prayer, which is prayed by all.

MORNING

C **I thank You, my heavenly Father, through Jesus Christ, Your dear Son, that You have kept me this night from all harm and danger; and I pray that You would keep me this day also from sin and every evil, that all my doings and life may please You. For into Your hands I commend myself, my body and soul, and all things. Let Your holy angel be with me, that the evil foe may have no power over me. Amen.**

EVENING

Ⓒ **I thank You, my heavenly Father, through Jesus Christ, Your dear Son, that You have graciously kept me this day; and I pray that You would forgive me all my sins where I have done wrong, and graciously keep me this night. For into Your hands I commend myself, my body and soul, and all things. Let Your holy angel be with me, that the evil foe may have no power over me. Amen.**

BENEDICAMUS AND BLESSING

Ⓛ Let us bless the Lord.

Ⓒ **Thanks be to God.**

Ⓛ The Lord bless us, defend us from all evil, and bring us to everlasting life.

Ⓒ **Amen.**

DAILY PRAYER
FOR INDIVIDUALS AND FAMILIES

These brief services may guide the daily prayer of individuals and families as well as in other settings.

When more than one person is present, the versicles and responses may be spoken responsively, with one person reading the words in regular type and the others responding with the words in **bold type**. Prayers may be prayed in the same fashion, though those in **bold type** are to be prayed by all.

For the readings, several verses have been recommended for each particular time of day. These may be used on a rotating basis. The value in using these few texts lies in the opportunity to learn them well. For those desiring a more complete selection of readings, daily lectionaries, such as those found in *Lutheran Worship,* pp. 295–99, *Lutheran Worship Altar Book,* pp. 133–36, or *The Lutheran Hymnal,* pp. 161–64, may be used. Readings from the Small Catechism can also be incorporated into the services.

In the prayers "for others and ourselves," the following suggestions may assist in establishing a rhythm of daily and weekly prayer.

Sunday:	For the joy of the resurrection among us; for true and godly worship throughout the world; for the faithful preaching and hearing of God's Word
Monday:	For faith to live in the promises of Holy Baptism; for one's calling and daily work; for the unemployed; for the salvation and well-being of our neighbors; for government; for peace
Tuesday:	For deliverance against temptation; for the addicted and despairing, the tortured and oppressed; for those struggling with sin
Wednesday:	For marriage and family, that all may live together under the grace of Christ according to the Word of God; for adults who must rear their children alone; for godly schools, church schools, and seminaries
Thursday:	For the Church and her pastors; for missionaries; for fruitful and salutary use of the sacrament of Christ's body and blood
Friday:	For the preaching of the cross of our Lord Jesus Christ and for its spread throughout the whole world, especially our community; for the persecuted; for the sick and dying
Saturday:	For faithfulness to the end; for the renewal of those who are withering in the faith or have fallen away; for receptive hearts and minds to God's Word on the Lord's Day; for pastors and people as they prepare to receive Christ's gifts

MORNING

The sign of the cross may be made by all in remembrance of their Baptism.

In the name of the Father and of the ✠ Son and of the Holy Spirit.
Amen.

O Lord, open my lips,
and my mouth will declare Your praise.   *Psalm 51:15*

In the morning, O Lord, You hear my voice;
in the morning I lay my requests before You
and wait in expectation.   *Psalm 5:3*

Glory be to the Father and to the Son and to the Holy Spirit;
as it was in the beginning, is now, and will be forever. Amen.

A hymn, canticle, or psalm may be sung or said.

READING

Since you have been raised with Christ, set your hearts on things above, where
Christ is seated at the right hand of God. Set your minds on things above, not
on earthly things. For you died, and your life is now hidden with Christ in God.
When Christ, who is your life, appears, then you will appear with Him in glory.

Colossians 3:1–4

*Other readings: Exodus 15:1–11; Isaiah 12:1–6; Matthew 20:1–16; Mark 13:32–36;
Luke 24:1–8; John 21:4–14; Ephesians 4:17–24; Romans 6:1–4.*

The Apostles' Creed (p. 25) may be confessed.

PRAYERS

- *Lord's Prayer*
- *Prayers for others and ourselves*
- *Concluding collect:*

Almighty God, merciful Father, who created and completed all things, on this day when the work of our calling begins anew, we implore You to create its beginning, direct its continuance, and bless its end, that our doings may be preserved from sin, our life sanctified, and our work this day be well pleasing to You; through Jesus Christ, our Lord. **Amen.**

I thank You, my heavenly Father, through Jesus Christ, Your dear Son, that You have kept me this night from all harm and danger; and I pray that You would keep me this day also from sin and every evil, that all my doings and life may please You. For into Your hands I commend myself, my body and soul, and all things. Let Your holy angel be with me, that the evil foe may have no power over me. Amen.

Small Catechism

Then go joyfully to your work.

29

NOON

The sign of the cross may be made by all in remembrance of their Baptism.

In the name of the Father and of the ✠ Son and of the Holy Spirit.
Amen.

Listen to my prayer, O God, do not ignore my plea;
hear my prayer and answer me.

Evening, morning, and noon
I cry out in distress and He hears my voice.

Cast your cares on the Lord and He will sustain you;
He will never let the righteous fall.   *Psalm 55:1, 16-17, 22*

**Glory be to the Father and to the Son and to the Holy Spirit;
as it was in the beginning, is now, and will be forever. Amen.**

A hymn, canticle, or psalm may be sung or said.

READING

Only, let everyone lead the life which the Lord has assigned to him, and in which God has called him. You were bought with a price; do not become slaves of men. So, brethren, in whatever state each was called, there let him remain with God.

1 Corinthians 7:17a, 23–24

It was now about the sixth hour, and darkness came over the whole land until the ninth hour, for the sun stopped shining. And the curtain of the temple was torn in two. Jesus called out with a loud voice, "Father, into Your hands I commit My spirit." When He had said this, He breathed His last.

Luke 23:44-46

*Other readings: Matthew 5:13–16; Matthew 13:1–9, 18–23; Mark 13:23–27;
John 15:1–9; Romans 7:18–25; Romans 12:1–2; 1 Peter 1:3–9; Revelation 7:13–17.*

PRAYERS

- *Lord's Prayer*
- *Prayers for others and ourselves*
- *Concluding collect:*

Blessed Savior, at this hour You hung upon the cross, stretching out Your loving arms. Grant that all the peoples of the earth may look to You and be saved; for Your mercy's sake. **Amen.**

Heavenly Father, send Your Holy Spirit into our hearts, to direct and rule us according to Your will, to comfort us in all our afflictions, to defend us from all error, and to lead us into all truth; through Jesus Christ, our Lord. **Amen.**

EARLY EVENING

Before or after the evening meal

The sign of the cross may be made by all in remembrance of their Baptism.

In the name of the Father and of the ☩ Son and of the Holy Spirit.
Amen.

A candle on the family altar or dinner table may be lighted.

Joyous light of glory of the immortal Father;
 heavenly, holy, blessed Jesus Christ.
We have come to the setting of the sun, and we look
 to the evening light.
We sing to God, the Father, Son, and Holy Spirit:
 You are worthy of being praised with pure voices forever.
O Son of God, O giver of life: the universe proclaims Your glory.

A hymn, canticle, or psalm may be sung or said.

READING

As they approached the village to which they were going, Jesus acted as if He were going farther. But they urged Him strongly, "Stay with us, for it is nearly evening; the day is almost over." So He went in to stay with them. When He was at the table with them, He took bread, gave thanks, broke it and began to give it to them. Then their eyes were opened and they recognized Him, and He disappeared from their sight. *Luke 24:28–31*

Other readings: Exodus 16:11–21, 31; Isaiah 25:6–9; Matthew 14:15–21; Matthew 27:57–60; Luke 14:15–24; John 6:25–35; John 10:7–18; Ephesians 6:10–18.

The Apostles' Creed (p. 25) may be confessed.

PRAYERS

- *Lord's Prayer*

- *Prayers for asking a blessing and returning thanks at mealtime:*

Lord God, heavenly Father, bless us and these Your gifts which we receive from Your bountiful goodness, through Jesus Christ, our Lord. Amen.

We thank You, Lord God, heavenly Father, through Jesus Christ, our Lord, for all Your benefits, who lives and reigns with You forever and ever. Amen.

- *Concluding collect:*

Lord Jesus, stay with us, for the evening is at hand and the day is past. Be our companion in the way, kindle our hearts, and awaken hope among us, that we may know You as You are revealed in Scripture and in the breaking of bread. Grant this for the sake of Your love. **Amen.**

CLOSE OF THE DAY
At bedtime

The sign of the cross may be made by all in remembrance of their Baptism.

In the name of the Father and of the ✠ Son and of the Holy Spirit.
Amen.

The Lord Almighty grant us a quiet night and peace at the last.
Amen.

It is good to give thanks to the Lord,
to sing praise to Your name, O Most High;

To herald Your love in the morning,
Your truth at the close of the day.

READING

Come to Me, all you who are weary and burdened, and I will give you rest.
Take My yoke upon you and learn from Me, for I am gentle and humble in
heart, and you will find rest for your souls. For My yoke is easy and My burden
is light.   *Matthew 11:28–30*

*Other readings: Micah 7:18–20; Matthew 18:15–35; Matthew 25:1–13; Luke 11:1–13;
Luke 12:13–34; Romans 8:31–39; 2 Corinthians 4:16–18; Revelation 21:22–22:5.*

CANTICLE

Lord, now You let Your servant go in peace; Your word has been fulfilled.
  My own eyes have seen the salvation
      which You have prepared in the sight of every people:
  a light to lighten the nations
      and the glory of Your people Israel.   *Luke 2:29–32*

**Glory be to the Father and to the Son and to the Holy Spirit;
as it was in the beginning, is now, and will be forever. Amen.**

PRAYERS

- *Lord's Prayer*
- *Prayers for others and ourselves*
- *Concluding collect:*

  **I thank You, my heavenly Father, through Jesus Christ, Your dear Son,
  that You have graciously kept me this day; and I pray that You would
  forgive me all my sins where I have done wrong, and graciously keep me
  this night. For into Your hands I commend myself, my body and soul, and
  all things. Let Your holy angel be with me, that the evil foe may have no
  power over me. Amen.**   *Small Catechism*

Then go to sleep at once and in good cheer.

PSALMS

PSALM 30

You turned my wail-ing in-to danc - ing;

I will give You thanks for - ev - er.

Psalm Tone *

¹I will exalt You, O Lord, for You lifted me out | of the depths*
and did not let my enemies gloat | over me.

²O Lord my God, I called to | You for help*
and You | healed me.

³O Lord, You brought me up | from the grave;*
You spared me from going down in- | to the pit.

Antiphon

⁴Sing to the Lord, You | saints of His;*
praise His | holy name.

⁵For His anger lasts only a moment, but His favor lasts a | lifetime;*
weeping may remain for a night, but rejoicing comes in the | morning.

Antiphon

⁶When I felt se- | cure, I said,*
"I shall never be | shaken."

⁷O Lord, when You favored me, You made my mountain | stand firm;*
but when You hid Your face, I | was dismayed.

⁸To You, O | Lord, I called;*
to the Lord I cried for | mercy:

⁹"What gain is there in my destruction, if I go down in- | to the pit?*
Will the dust praise You? Will it proclaim Your | faithfulness?

¹⁰Hear, O Lord, and be merci- | ful to me;*
O Lord, | be my help."

Antiphon

¹¹You turned my wailing into | dancing;*
You removed my sackcloth and clothed | me with joy,

¹²that my heart may sing to You and not be | silent.*
O Lord my God, I will give You thanks for- | ever.

Glory be to the Father and | to the Son*
and to the Holy | Spirit;

as it was in the be- | ginning,*
is now, and will be forever. | Amen.

Antiphon

PSALM 31

Let Your face———— shine—— on Your ser - vant,

and save me in Your un - fail - ing love.

¹In You, O Lord, I have taken refuge;
let me never be | put to shame;*
  deliver me in Your | righteousness.

²Turn Your ear to me, come quickly to
my | rescue;*
  be my rock of refuge, a strong
  fortress to | save me.

³Since You are my rock and
my | fortress,*
  for the sake of Your name lead
  and | guide me.

⁴Free me from the trap that is | set for
me,*
  for You are my | refuge.

⁵Into Your hands I commit my | spirit;*
  redeem me, O Lord, the | God of
  truth.

⁶I hate those who cling to
worthless | idols;*
  I trust | in the Lord.

⁷I will be glad and rejoice | in Your
love,*
  for You saw my affliction and knew
  the anguish | of my soul.

⁸You have not handed me over to
the | enemy*
  but have set my feet in a | spacious
  place.

Antiphon

⁹Be merciful to me, O Lord, for I
am | in distress;*
  my eyes grow weak with sorrow,
  my soul and my bod- | y with grief.

¹⁰My life is consumed by anguish and
my years by | groaning;*
  my strength fails because of my
  affliction, and my | bones grow
  weak.

¹¹Because of all my enemies, I am the
utter contempt of my | neighbors;*
  I am a dread to my friends—those
  who see me on the street | flee from
  me.

¹²I am forgotten by them as though | I
were dead;*
  I have become like broken | pottery.

¹³For I hear the slander of many; there
is terror on | every side;*
  they conspire against me and plot
  to | take my life.

¹⁴But I trust in | You, O Lord;*
  I say, "You | are my God."

Antiphon

¹⁵My times are | in Your hands;*
  deliver me from my enemies and
  from those who pur- | sue me.

¹⁶Let Your face shine on Your |
servant;*
  save me in Your un- | failing love.

¹⁷Let me not be put to shame, O Lord,
for I have cried | out to You;*
  but let the wicked be put to shame
  and lie silent | in the grave.

¹⁸Let their lying lips be | silenced,*
  for with pride and contempt they
  speak arrogantly against
  the | righteous.

¹⁹How great is Your goodness, which
You have stored up for those
who | fear You,*
  which You bestow in the sight of
  men on those who take ref- | uge in
  You.

²⁰In the shelter of Your presence You
hide them from the in- | trigues of
men;*
  in Your dwelling You keep them safe
  from the | strife of tongues.

Antiphon

²¹Praise be | to the Lord,*
  for He showed His wonderful love to
  me when I was in a besieged | city.

²²In my alarm I said, "I am cut off |
from Your sight!"*
  Yet You heard my cry for mercy
  when I called to | You for help.

²³Love the Lord, | all His saints*
  The Lord preserves the faithful, but
  the proud He pays | back in full.

²⁴Be strong | and take heart,*
  all you who hope | in the Lord.

**Glory be to the Father and | to the
Son***
  and to the Holy | Spirit;

as it was in the be- | ginning,*
  is now, and will be forever. | Amen.

Antiphon

PSALM 33

We wait— in— hope for the Lord;— He is our help and our shield.

¹Sing joyfully to the Lord,
you | righteous; *
  it is fitting for the upright to | praise
Him.

²Praise the Lord | with the harp; *
  make music to Him on the | ten-
stringed lyre.

³Sing to Him a | new song; *
  play skillfully, and | shout for joy.

⁴For the Word of the Lord is | right and
true; *
  He is faithful in | all He does.

Antiphon

⁵The Lord loves righteousness
and | justice; *
  the earth is full of His un- | failing
love.

⁶By the Word of the Lord were
the | heavens made, *
  their starry host by the breath | of His
mouth.

⁷He gathers the waters of the sea | into
jars; *
  He puts the deep into | storehouses.

⁸Let all the earth | fear the Lord; *
  let all the people of the world
re- | vere Him.

⁹For He spoke, and it | came to be; *
  He commanded, and | it stood firm.

¹⁰The Lord foils the plans of
the | nations; *
  He thwarts the purposes of
the | peoples.

¹¹But the plans of the Lord stand firm
for- | ever, *
  the purposes of His heart through all
gener- | ations.

¹²Blessed is the nation whose God | is
the Lord, *
  the people He chose for His
in- | heritance.

Antiphon

¹³From heaven the | Lord looks down *
  and sees all | mankind;

¹⁴from His | dwelling place *
  He watches all who | live on earth—

¹⁵He who forms the | hearts of all, *
  who considers every- | thing they do.

¹⁶No king is saved by the size of
his | army; *
  no warrior escapes by his | great
strength.

Antiphon

¹⁷A horse is a vain hope for
de- | liverance; *
  despite all its great strength
it | cannot save.

[18]But the eyes of the Lord are on those
  who | fear Him,*
    on those whose hope is in His
    un- | failing love,

[19]to deliver | them from death*
    and keep them alive in | famine.

[20]We wait in hope | for the Lord;*
    He is our help | and our shield.

[21]In Him our | hearts rejoice,*
    for we trust in His | holy name.

[22]May Your unfailing love rest upon | us,
  O Lord,*
    even as we put our | hope in You.

**Glory be to the Father and | to the
Son***
  and to the Holy | Spirit;

as it was in the be- | ginning,*
  is now, and will be forever. | Amen.

Antiphon

PSALM 40

You are my help and my— sure de - fense; O my God, do not de - lay.

¹I waited patiently | for the Lord;*
  He turned to me and | heard my cry.

²He lifted me out of the slimy pit, out
of the | mud and mire;*
  He set my feet on a rock and gave
  me a firm | place to stand.

³He put a new song in my mouth, a
hymn of praise | to our God.*
  Many will see and fear and put their
  trust | in the Lord.

Antiphon

⁴Blessed is the man who makes
the | Lord his trust,*
  who does not look to the proud, to
  those who turn aside to | false gods.

⁵Many, O Lord my God, are the
wonders You have done. The things
You planned for us no one can
re- | count to You;*
  were I to speak and tell of them, they
  would be too many | to declare.

⁶Sacrifice and offering You did not
desire, but my ears | You have
pierced;*
  burnt offerings and sin offerings You
  did | not require.

⁷Then I said, "Here I am, | I have
come—*
  it is written about me | in the scroll.

⁸To do Your will, O my God is | my
desire*
  Your law is with- | in my heart."

Antiphon

⁹I proclaim righteousness in the great
as- | sembly;*
  I do not seal my lips, as You | know,
  O Lord.

¹⁰I do not hide Your righteousness in my
heart; I speak of Your faithfulness and
sal- | vation.*
  I do not conceal Your love and Your
  truth from the great as- | sembly.

¹¹Do not withhold Your mercy from | me,
O Lord;*
  may Your love and Your truth always
  pro- | tect me.

¹²For troubles without number surround
me; my sins have overtaken me, and
I | cannot see.*
  They are more than the hairs of my
  head, and my heart fails with- | in me.

Antiphon

¹³Be pleased, O Lord, to | save me;*
  O Lord, come quickly to | help me.

¹⁴May all who seek to take my life be
put to shame and con- | fusion;*
  may all who desire my ruin be turned
  back | in disgrace.

[15]May those who say to me, "A- | ha! Aha!"*
   be appalled at their | own shame.

[16]But may all who seek You rejoice and be | glad in You;*
   may those who love Your salvation
   always say, "The Lord be ex- | alted!"

[17]Yet I am poor and | needy;*
   may the Lord | think of me.

[18]You are my help and my de- | liverer;*
   O my God, do | not delay.

Glory be to the Father and | to the Son*
   and to the Holy | Spirit;

as it was in the be- | ginning,*
   is now, and will be forever. | Amen.

Antiphon

PSALM 42

My soul thirsts for God, for the liv - ing God.____

¹As the deer pants for streams
of | water,*
  so my soul pants for | You, O God.

²My soul thirsts for God, for the | living
God.*
  When can I go and | meet with God?

³My tears have been my food | day and
night,*
  while men say to me all day long,
  "Where | is your God?"

⁴These things I remember as I pour | out
my soul:*
  how I used to go with the multitude,
  leading the procession to the | house
  of God,
with shouts of joy and thanks- | giving*
  among the | festive throng.

Antiphon

⁵Why are you downcast, | O my soul?*
  Why so disturbed with- | in me?
Put your | hope in God,*
  for I will yet praise Him, my
  Savior | and my God.

⁶My soul is downcast with- | in me;*
  therefore I will remember You from
  the land of the Jordan, the heights of
  Hermon—from Mount | Mizar.

⁷Deep calls to deep in the roar of
Your | waterfalls;*
  all Your waves and breakers have
  swept | over me.

Antiphon

⁸By day the Lord di- | rects His love,*
  at night His song is with me—a
  prayer to the God | of my life.

⁹I say to God my Rock, "Why have You
for- | gotten me?*
  Why must I go about mourning,
  oppressed by the | enemy?"

¹⁰My bones suffer mortal agony as my
foes | taunt me,*
  saying to me all day long, "Where | is
  your God?"

Antiphon

¹¹Why are you downcast, | O my soul?*
  Why so disturbed with- | in me?
Put your | hope in God,*
  for I will yet praise Him, my
  Savior | and my God.

**Glory be to the Father and | to the
Son***
  and to the Holy | Spirit;

as it was in the be- | ginning,*
  is now, and will be forever. | Amen.

Antiphon

PSALM 47

God has as-cend-ed with shouts of joy,_____ the

Lord a-mid the sound-ing of trum-pets._____

Psalm Tone *

¹Clap your hands, all you | nations;*
  shout to God with | cries of joy.

²How awesome is the | Lord Most High,*
  the great King over | all the earth!

³He subdued nations | under us,*
  peoples un- | der our feet.

⁴He chose our inheri- | tance for us,*
  the pride of Jacob, | whom He loved.

Antiphon

⁵God has ascended amid | shouts of joy,*
  the Lord amid the sounding of | trumpets.

⁶Sing praises to God, sing | praises;*
  sing praises to our King,
  sing | praises.

⁷For God is the King of | all the earth;*
  sing to Him a | psalm of praise.

Antiphon

⁸God reigns over the | nations;*
  God is seated on His | holy throne.

⁹The nobles of the nations assemble as the people of the God of | Abraham*
  for the kings of the earth belong to God; He is greatly ex- | alted.

Glory be to the Father and | to the Son*
  and to the Holy | Spirit;

as it was in the be- | ginning,*
  is now, and will be forever. | Amen.

Antiphon

PSALM 85

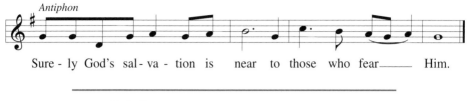

Sure - ly God's sal - va - tion is   near   to those   who fear_____ Him.

Psalm Tone

¹You showed favor to Your | land, O
Lord;*
　　You restored the fortunes of | Jacob.

²You forgave the iniquity of
Your | people*
　　and covered | all their sins.

³You set aside | all Your wrath*
　　and turned from Your fierce | anger.

Antiphon

⁴Restore us again, O God our | Savior,*
　　and put away Your displeasure |
　　towards us.

⁵Will You be angry with us for- | ever?*
　　Will You prolong Your anger through
　　all gener- | ations?

⁶Will You not revive | us again,*
　　that Your people may re- | joice in
　　You?

⁷Show us Your unfailing | love, O
Lord,*
　　and grant us Your sal- | vation.

Antiphon

⁸I will listen to what God the | Lord
will say;*
　　He promises peace to His people, His
　　saints—but let them not return
　　to | folly.

⁹Surely His salvation is near those
who | fear Him,*
　　that His glory may dwell | in our
　　land.

¹⁰Love and faithfulness meet
to- | gether;*
　　righteousness and peace kiss
　　each | other.

¹¹Faithfulness springs forth | from the
earth,*
　　and righteousness looks down
　　from | heaven.

Antiphon

¹²The Lord will indeed give | what is
good,*
　　and our land will yield its | harvest.

¹³Righteousness goes be- | fore Him*
　　and prepares the way | for His steps.

**Glory be to the Father and | to the
Son***
　　and to the Holy | Spirit;

as it was in the be- | ginning,*
　　is now, and will be forever. | Amen.

Antiphon

PSALM 97

Antiphon (General)

Re - joice in the Lord, you— righ - teous, and praise His ho - ly name.

Antiphon (Christmas)

To us a child is born,——————— to us a Son— is giv'n.—

Psalm Tone

¹The Lord reigns, let the | earth be
glad;*
  let the distant | shores rejoice.

²Clouds and thick darkness sur- | round
Him;*
  righteousness and justice are the
  foundation | of His throne.

³Fire goes be- | fore Him*
  and consumes His foes on | every
  side.

⁴His lightning lights | up the world;*
  the earth sees and | trembles.

⁵The mountains melt like wax be- | fore
the Lord,*
  before the Lord of | all the earth.

Antiphon

⁶The heavens proclaim His | righ-
teousness,*
  and all the peoples see His | glory.

⁷All who worship images are | put to
shame,*
  those who boast in idols—worship
  Him, | all you gods!

⁸Zion hears and rejoices and the
villages of Ju- | dah are glad*
  because of Your judg- | ments, O
  Lord.

⁹For You, O Lord, are the Most High
over | all the earth;*
  You are exalted far a- | bove all gods.

Antiphon

¹⁰Let those who love the Lord
hate | evil,*
  for He guards the lives of His faithful
  ones and delivers them from the hand
  of the | wicked.

¹¹Light is shed upon the | righteous*
  and joy on the up- | right in heart.

¹²Rejoice in the Lord, you who
are | righteous*
  and praise His | holy name.

**Glory be to the Father and | to the
Son***
  and to the Holy | Spirit;

as it was in the be- | ginning,*
  is now, and will be forever. | Amen.

Antiphon

PSALM 99

Great is the Lord in— Zi-on; He is ex-alt-ed o-ver all the na-tions.

¹The Lord reigns, let the
nations | tremble;*
  He sits enthroned between the
  cherubim, let the | earth shake.

²Great is the Lord in | Zion;*
  He is exalted over all the | nations.

³Let them praise Your great
and | awesome name—*
  He is | holy.

⁴The King is mighty, He loves justice—
You have established | equity;*
  in Jacob You have done what is | just
  and right.

Antiphon

⁵Exalt the | Lord our God*
  and worship at His footstool;
  He is | holy.

⁶Moses and Aaron were among His
priests, Samuel was among those who
called | on His name;*
  they called on the Lord and
  He | answered them.

⁷He spoke to them from the pil- | lar of
cloud;*
  they kept His statutes and the decrees
  He | gave them.

⁸O Lord our God, You | answered
them;*
  You were to Israel a forgiving God,
  though You punished their | misdeeds.

Antiphon

⁹Exalt the Lord our God and worship at
His holy | mountain,*
  for the Lord our God is | holy.

**Glory be to the Father and | to the
Son***
  and to the Holy | Spirit;

as it was in the be- | ginning,*
  is now, and will be forever. | Amen.

Antiphon

PSALM 112

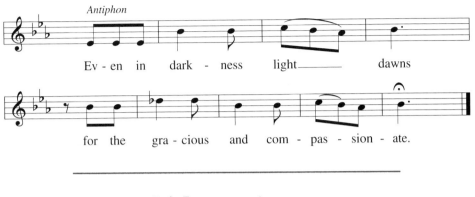

Ev - en in dark - ness light_____ dawns

for the gra - cious and com - pas - sion - ate.

Psalm Tone *

¹Praise the Lord. Blessed is the man who | fears the Lord,*
  who finds great delight in | His commands.

²His children will be mighty | in the land:*
  each generation of the upright | will be blessed.

³Wealth and riches are | in his house,*
  and his righteousness endures for- | ever.

⁴Even in darkness light dawns for the | upright,*
  for the gracious and compassionate and | righteous man.

Antiphon

⁵Good will come to him who is generous and lends | freely,*
  who conducts his affairs with | justice.

⁶Surely he will never be | shaken;*
  a righteous man will be remembered for- | ever.

⁷He will have no fear of | bad news;*
  his heart is steadfast, trusting | in the Lord.

⁸His heart is secure, he will | have no fear;*
  in the end he will look in triumph | on his foes.

Antiphon

⁹He has scattered abroad his gifts | to the poor,*
  his righteousness endures forever; his horn will be lifted high in | honor.

¹⁰The wicked man will see and be vexed, he will gnash his teeth and | waste away;*
  the longings of the wicked will come to | nothing.

Glory be to the Father and | to the Son*
  and to the Holy | Spirit;

as it was in the be- | ginning,*
  is now, and will be forever. | Amen.

Antiphon

PSALM 141

Let my prayer be set— be - fore You as in - cense.

Psalm Tone

[1]O Lord, I call to You; come
quick- | ly to me.*
　Hear my voice when I | call to
　You.

[2]May my prayer be set before You
like | incense;*
　may the lifting up of my hands be
　like the evening | sacrifice.

Antiphon

[3]Set a guard over my | mouth, O Lord;*
　keep watch over the door | of my lips.

[4]Let not my heart be drawn to what is
evil, to take part in wicked deeds with
men who are evil- | doers;*
　let me not eat of their del- | icacies.

Antiphon

[5]Let a righteous man strike me—it is a
kindness; let him rebuke me—it is
oil | on my head.*
　My head will not refuse it.
　Yet my prayer is ever against the
　deeds of evil- | doers;

[6]their rulers will be thrown down | from
the cliffs,*
　and the wicked will learn that
　my words were well | spoken.

[7]They will say, "As one plows and
breaks | up the earth,*
　so our bones have been scattered at
　the mouth | of the grave."

[8]But my eyes are fixed on You,
O | Sovereign Lord;*
　in You I take refuge—do not
　give me o- | ver to death.

Antiphon

[9]Keep me from the snares they
have | laid for me,*
　from the traps set by evil- | doers.

[10]Let the wicked fall into their | own
nets,*
　while I pass by in | safety.

**Glory be to the Father and | to the
Son***
　and to the Holy | Spirit;

as it was in the be- | ginning,*
　is now, and will be forever. | Amen.

Antiphon

Rejoice, Rejoice, Believers

801

1 Re - joice, re - joice, be - liev - ers, And let your lights ap - pear;
2 The watch-ers on the moun - tain Pro - claim the bride-groom near;
3 The saints, who here in pa - tience Their cross and suf - f'rings bore,
4 Our hope and ex - pec - ta - tion, O Je - sus, now ap - pear;

The eve-ning is ad - vanc - ing, And dark - er night is near.
Go forth as He ap - proach - es With al - le - lu - ias clear.
Shall live and reign for - ev - er When sor - row is no more.
A - rise, O Sun so longed for, O'er this be - night - ed sphere.

The bride-groom is a - ris - ing And soon is draw-ing nigh.
The mar - riage feast is wait - ing; The gates wide o - pen stand.
A - round the throne of glo - ry The Lamb they shall be - hold;
With hearts and hands up - lift - ed, We plead, O Lord, to see

Up, pray and watch and wres - tle; At mid - night comes the cry.
A - rise, O heirs of glo - ry; The bride-groom is at hand.
In tri - umph cast be - fore Him Their di - a - dems of gold.
The day of earth's re - demp - tion That sets Your peo - ple free!

Text: Laurentius Laurenti, 1660–1722; tr. Sarah B. Findlater, 1823–1907, alt.
Tune: Swedish folk tune; setting: Ronald A. Nelson, b. 1927

Text and tune: Public domain
Setting: © 1978 *Lutheran Book of Worship*

HAF TRONES LAMPA FÄRDIG
76 76 D

Matt. 25:1–6; Rev. 5:11–14; Mal. 4:2

Lo! He Comes
with Clouds Descending

802

1 Lo! He comes with clouds de - scend - ing,
2 Ev - 'ry eye shall now be - hold Him
3 Those dear to - kens of His Pas - sion
4 Yea, a - men, let all a - dore Thee,

Once for ev - 'ry sin - ner slain;
Robed in glo - rious maj - es - ty;
Still His daz - zling bod - y bears,
High on Thine e - ter - nal throne;

Thou - sand thou - sand saints at - tend - ing
Those who set at nought and sold Him,
Cause of end - less ex - ul - ta - tion
Sav - ior, take the pow'r and glo - ry,

Swell the tri - umph of His train:
Pierced and nailed Him to the tree,
To His ran - somed wor - ship - ers.
Claim the king - dom as Thine own.

While this text is already a familiar one through its inclusion in Lutheran Worship,
it appears here with this vigorous tune used by many other Christians.

Text: Charles Wesley, 1707–88, alt.
Tune: Thomas Olivers, 1725–99; setting: Ralph Vaughan Williams, 1872–1958, alt.

HELMSLEY
87 87 12 7

Text and music: Public domain

Rev. 1:7; 19:11–16

Al - le - lu - ia, al - le - lu - ia, al - le -
Deep - ly wail - ing, deep - ly wail - ing, deep - ly
With what rap - ture, with what rap - ture, with what
Al - le - lu - ia, al - le - lu - ia, al - le -

lu - ia! Christ the Lord re - turns to reign.
wail - ing, Shall their true Mes - si - ah see.
rap - ture Gaze we on those glo - rious scars!
lu - ia! Thou shalt reign, and Thou a - lone!

Magnificat 803

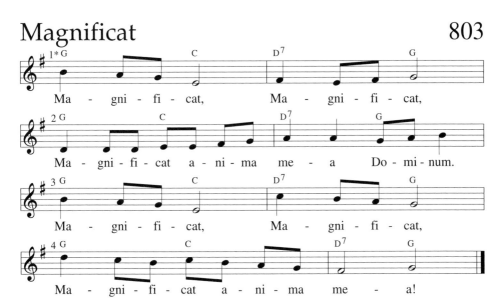

1* Ma - gni - fi - cat, Ma - gni - fi - cat,

2 Ma - gni - fi - cat a - ni - ma me - a Do - mi - num.

3 Ma - gni - fi - cat, Ma - gni - fi - cat,

4 Ma - gni - fi - cat a - ni - ma me - a!

May be sung as a two-, three-, or four-part canon.

Magnificat anima mea Dominum (Mahg-NIF-ee-kaht AH-nee-mah MAY-ah DOH-mee-noom):
My soul magnifies the Lord.

Text: Luke 1:46
Music: Jacques Berthier, 1923–94

MAGNIFICAT
Irregular

Luke 1:46

804 Lift Up Your Heads, O Gates

1 Lift up your heads, O gates; The King of glory waits. Lift high, O an-cient doors, o-bey; Pre-pare the roy-al way.

2 Who is this glo-ri-ous King Whose praise the na-tions sing? The Lord, the Might-y, Ho-ly One, Whose strength the vic-t'ry won.

3 Lift up your heads, O gates; The King of glory waits. Lift high, O an-cient doors, o-bey; Pre-pare the roy-al way.

Refrain

Ho - san - na, ho - san - na! Re - joice, give thanks, and sing!

Psalm 24 invites us to greet the coming King of Glory. This robust tune, with its rising melodic line and modulations, accentuates this announcement of our Lord's arrival.

Text: Bert Polman, b. 1945
Music: Richard W. Dirksen, b. 1921

Text: © 1987 CRC Publications
Music: © 1974 Harold Flammer Music, a div. of Shawnee Press, Inc.

VINEYARD HAVEN
SM and refrain

Ps. 24:7–10; Matt. 21:9

The Angel Gabriel
from Heaven Came

1 The an - gel Ga - bri - el from heav - en came,
2 "For know a bless - ed moth - er thou shalt be,
3 Then gen - tle Mar - y meek - ly bowed her head;
4 Of her, Em-man - u - el, the Christ, was born

With wings as drift - ed snow, with eyes as flame:
All gen - er - a - tions laud and hon - or thee;
"To me be as it pleas - eth God," she said.
In Beth - le - hem all on a Christ - mas morn,

"All hail to thee, O low - ly maid - en Mar - y,
Thy son shall be Em - man - u - el, by seers fore - told,
"My soul shall laud and mag - ni - fy God's ho - ly name."
And Chris - tian folk through-out the world will ev - er say:

Most high - ly fa - vored la - dy."
Most high - ly fa - vored la - dy."   Glo - ri - a!
Most high - ly fa - vored la - dy,
"Most high - ly fa - vored la - dy,"

Text: Basque carol, para. Sabine Baring-Gould, 1834–1924
Tune: Basque carol; setting: C. Edgar Pettman, 1865–1943 and John Wickham

Text and tune: Public domain
Setting: © 1955 (Renewal 1983), E. H. Freeman, Ltd., admin. by Glenwood Music Corp.

GABRIEL'S MESSAGE

Luke 1:26–38; Is. 7:14

806 The Night Will Soon Be Ending

1 The night will soon be ending; The
2 The One whom an - gels tend - ed Comes
3 The earth in sure ro - ta - tion Will
4 Yet nights will bring their sad - ness And

dawn can - not be far. Let songs of praise as -
near, a child, to serve; Thus God, the judge of -
soon bring morn - ing bright, So run where God's sal -
rob our hearts of peace; And sin in all its

cend - ing Now greet the Morn - ing Star!
fend - ed, Bears all our sins de - serve.
va - tion Glows in a sta - ble's light.
mad - ness A - round us may in - crease.

All you whom dark - ness fright - ens With
The guilt - y need not cow - er, For
As old as sin's per - ver - sion Is
But now one Star is beam - ing Whose

Text: Jochen Klepper, 1903–42; tr. Herman G. Stuempfle, Jr., b. 1923
Tune: Welsh folk tune; setting: Ralph Vaughan Williams, 1872–1958
Translation: © 1998 GIA Publications, Inc.
Music: Public domain

LLANGLOFFAN
76 76 D

Rom. 13:12a; Rev. 22:16–17; 1 Cor. 2:7; John 1:4–5; 3:19–21

guilt or grief or pain, God's ra - diant Star now
God has rec - on - ciled Through His re - demp - tive
mer - cy's vast de - sign: God brings a new cre -
rays have pierced the night: God comes for our re -

bright - ens And bids you sing a - gain.
pow - er All those who trust this child.
a - tion— This child its seal and sign.
deem - ing From sin's op - press - ive might.

5 God dwells with us in darkness
   And spreads His light abroad;
   But we resist the brightness
   And turn away from God.

Yet grace does not forsake us
   Though far from home we run.
   His children God has made us
   Through His beloved Son.

Prepare the Way 807

Capo 1 (D) (G) (D)
1* E♭ A♭ E♭

Pre - pare the way of the Lord. Pre -

(D) (G) (D) (D) (G)
2 E♭ A♭ E♭ 3 E♭ A♭

pare the way of the Lord, and all peo - ple will

(D) (D) (D)
E♭ 4 E♭ A♭ E♭

see the sal - va - tion of our God. Pre -

May be sung as a two-, three-, or four-part canon.

Text: Luke 3:4, 6
Music: Jacques Berthier, 1923–94

THE WAY
Irregular

Luke 3:4, 6; Is. 40:3–5

808 See in Yonder Manger Low

1 See in yon-der man - ger low, Born for us on earth be - low,
2 Lo, with - in a sta - ble lies He who built the star - ry skies,
3 Sa - cred In - fant, all di - vine, What a ten-der love was Thine,
4 Teach, oh, teach us, ho - ly Child, By Thy face so meek and mild,

See— the gen - tle Lamb ap-pears, Prom-ised from e - ter - nal years.
He who, throned in height sub-lime, Sits a - mid the cher - u - bim.
Thus to come from high - est bliss Down to such a world as this.
Teach us to re - sem - ble Thee In Thy sweet hu - mil - i - ty.

Refrain

Hail, O ev - er - bless-ed morn; Hail re-demp-tion's hap - py dawn;

Sing through all Je - ru - sa-lem: "Christ is born in Beth-le-hem!"

Text: Edward Caswall, 1814–78, alt.
Music: John Goss, 1800–80

Text and music: Public domain

HUMILITY
77 77 with Refrain

Luke 2:1–20; John 1:29; Phil. 2:3–11

On This Day Earth Shall Ring 809

1 On this day earth shall ring With the song chil-dren sing
2 His the doom, ours the mirth; When He came down to earth,
3 God's bright star, o'er His head, Wise men three to Him led,
4 On this day an-gels sing; With their song earth shall ring,

To the Lord, Christ our King, Born on earth to save us;
Beth-le-hem saw His birth; Ox and ass be-side Him
Kneel they low by His bed, Lay their gifts be-fore Him,
Prais-ing Christ, heav-en's King, Born on earth to save us;

Refrain

God in Him for-gave us.
From the cold would hide Him.
Praise Him and a-dore Him.
Peace and love He gave us.

I - de-o - o - o,

i-de-o - o - o, i-de-o glo-ri-a in ex-cel-sis De-o!

This strong tune frames this Christmas text's staccatolike phrases. "Ideo (EE-day-OH) gloria in excelsis Deo!" is Latin for "Therefore, glory to God in the highest!"

Text: *Piae Cantiones*, 1582; tr. Jane Joseph, 1894–1929
Tune: *Piae Cantiones*, 1582; setting: Steven F. Wente, b. 1952

Text and tune: Public domain
Setting: © 1998 Concordia Publishing House

PERSONENT HODIE
666 66 and refrain

Luke 2:1–20; Matt. 2:1–12

810 A Stable Lamp Is Lighted

1 A sta - ble lamp is light - ed Whose
2 (This) child through Da - vid's ci - ty Shall
3 (Yet) He shall be for - sak - en, And
4 (But) now, as at the end - ing, The

glow shall wake the sky; The stars shall bend their voic - es, And
ride in tri - umph by; The palm shall strew its branch - es, And
yield - ed up to die; The sky shall groan and dark - en, And
low is lift - ed high; The stars shall bend their voic - es, And

ev - 'ry stone shall cry. And ev - 'ry stone shall
ev - 'ry stone shall cry. And ev - 'ry stone shall
ev - 'ry stone shall cry. And ev - 'ry stone shall
ev - 'ry stone shall cry. And ev - 'ry stone shall

Christ's birth culminates in His death and resurrection. Even the very stones of creation praise
God for such redemptive love. This message is here further underscored by the poignant tune.

Text: Richard Wilbur, b. 1921
Music: David Hurd, b. 1950

ANDÚJAR
76 76 66 76

Text: "A Christmas Hymn" from ADVICE TO A PROPHET AND OTHER POEMS, copyright © 1961
and renewed 1989 by Richard Wilbur, reprinted by permission of Harcourt Brace & Company.
Music: © 1984 GIA Publications, Inc.

Luke 2:6–7; 19:37–40; 2 Cor. 5:18

cry,   And   straw   like gold   shall   shine;   A
cry.   Though   heav -   y,   dull,   and   dumb,   And
cry,   For   ston -   y   hearts   of   men: God's
cry,   In   prais -   es   of   the   Child   By

barn shall har - bor   heav - en,   A   stall   be - come   a
lie   with - in   the   road - way   To pave   His king - dom
blood up - on   the   spear - head,   God's love   re - fused   a -
whose de - scent   a -   mong   us   The worlds   are rec -   on -

shrine.
come.
gain.
ciled.

1–3

2 This
3 Yet
4 But

Break Forth, O Beauteous Heavenly Light

811

1 Break forth, O beau - teous heav'n - ly light, And ush - er in the morn - ing. Ye shep-herds, shrink not with af-fright, The day of grace is dawn - ing. This Child, though weak in in - fan - cy, Our con - fi - dence and

2 O dear - est Child, whom I a - dore, Whose grace sur - pass - es mea - sure, My Broth - er, whom I cher - ish more Than earth with all its trea - sure: Haste from Thy man - ger to de - part, O come and dwell with -

3 All bless - ing, thanks, and praise to Thee, Lord Je - sus Christ, be giv - en: Thou hast my Broth - er deigned to be, Thou Lord of earth and heav - en. Help me through-out this day of grace To praise Thy love and

This chorale from J. S. Bach's Christmas Oratorio proclaims the birth of the Christ Child for our salvation. By His death and resurrection, Christ our brother has broken the power of Satan and made peace between us and the Father.

Text: Johann Rist, 1607–67; tr. *Lutheran Hymnal* (Australia)
Tune: Johann Schop, c. 1595–c. 1667; setting: Johann S. Bach, 1685–1750

ERMUNTRE DICH
87 87 88 77

Text: © 1973 *Lutheran Hymnal*, Openbook Publishers
Music: Public domain

Is. 9:2–7; 1 Tim. 2:5; John 1:1–5, 14; Eph. 2:14

joy shall be, The pow'r of Sa - tan
in my heart; With joy will I re -
seek Thy face; And when I stand be -

break - ing, Our peace with God now mak - ing.
ceive Thee, A cra - dle there will give Thee.
fore Thee For - ev - er to a - dore Thee.

812

Infant Holy, Infant Lowly

1 In - fant ho - ly, in - fant low - ly, For His bed a cat - tle stall;
2 Flocks were sleep-ing, shep-herds keep-ing Vig - il till the morn-ing new

Ox - en low - ing, lit - tle know-ing Christ the child is Lord of all.
Saw the glo - ry, heard the sto - ry, Tid - ings of a Gos-pel true.

Swift-ly wing-ing, an - gels sing-ing, Bells are ring-ing, tid-ings bring-ing:
Thus re - joic-ing, free from sor-row, Prais - es voic-ing, greet the mor-row:

Christ the child is Lord of all! Christ the child is Lord of all!
Christ the child was born for you! Christ the child was born for you!

Text: Polish carol; tr. Edith M. G. Reed, 1885–1933, alt.
Tune: Polish carol; setting: Richard W. Hillert, b. 1923

Text and tune: Public domain
Setting: © 1978 Lutheran Book of Worship

W ZLOBIE LEZY
87 87 88 77

Luke 2:1–20

Where Shepherds Lately Knelt 813

1 Where shep-herds late-ly knelt and kept the an-gel's word,
2 In that un-like-ly place I find Him as they said:
3 How should I not have known I-sa-iah would be there,
4 Can I, will I for-get how Love was born, and burned

I come in half-be-lief, a pil-grim strange-ly stirred;
Sweet new-born babe, how frail! and in a man-ger bed:
His proph-e-cies ful-filled? With pound-ing heart I stare:
Its way in-to my heart— un-asked, un-forced, un-earned,

But there is room and wel-come there for me,
A still, small voice to cry one day for me,
A child, a son, the Prince of Peace for me,
To die, to live, and not a-lone for me,

But there is room and wel-come there for me.
A still, small voice to cry one day for me.
A child, a son, the Prince of Peace for me.
To die, to live, and not a-lone for me?

The picturesque language of this text invites the worshiper to consider Christ's birth in a very personal way, as if one were standing at the very manger of Jesus. The gentle melody is a perfect match for this Christmas hymn.

Text: Jaroslav J. Vajda, b. 1919
Music: Carl F. Schalk, b. 1929

Text: © 1987 Jaroslav J. Vajda
Music: © 1987 GIA Publications, Inc.

MANGER SONG
12 12 10 10

Luke 2:1–16; Is. 9:1–7

814 O Jesus Christ, Thy Manger Is

1 O Jesus Christ, Thy manger is My paradise at which my soul reclineth. For there, O Lord, Doth lie the Word Made flesh for us; herein Thy grace forth shineth.

2 He whom the sea And wind obey Doth come to serve the sinner in great meekness. Thou, God's own Son, With us art one, Dost join us and our children in our weakness.

3 Thy light and grace Our guilt efface, Thy heav'nly riches all our loss retrieving. Imanuel, Thy birth doth quell The pow'r of hell and Satan's bold deceiving.

4 Thou Christian heart, Who e'er thou art, Be of good cheer and let no sorrow move thee! For God's own Child, In mercy mild, Joins thee to Him; how greatly God must love thee!

The great Lutheran hymn writer Paul Gerhardt here invites the believer to treasure the incarnate Son of God above all earthly things. The familiar text is joined to a new tune by Kenneth Kosche of Mequon, Wisconsin.

Text: Paul Gerhardt, 1607–76; tr. composite, *The Lutheran Hymnal*, 1941
Music: Kenneth T. Kosche, b. 1947

IN PARADISUM
4 4 11 D

Luke 2:4–11; Matt. 1:21–23

5 Remember thou What glory now
   The Lord prepared
     thee for all earthly sadness.
   The angel host Can never boast
   Of greater glory,
     greater bliss or gladness.

6 The world may hold Her wealth and gold;
   But thou, my heart,
     keep Christ as thy true treasure.
   To Him hold fast Until at last
   A crown be thine
     and honor in full measure.

Christ, When for Us You Were Baptized

EPIPHANY

815

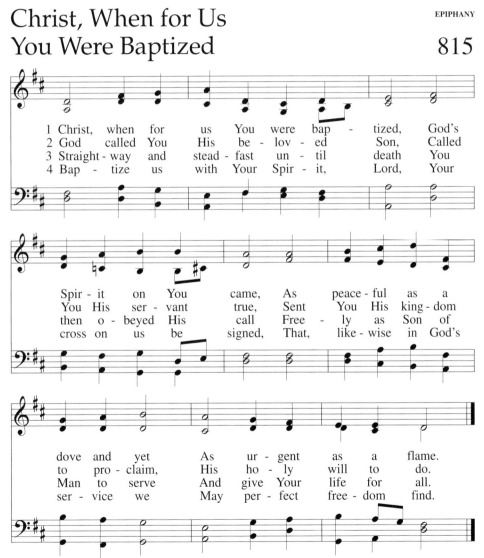

1 Christ, when for us You were bap - tized, God's Spir - it on You came, As peace - ful as a dove and yet As ur - gent as a flame.
2 God called You His be - lov - ed Son, Called You His ser - vant true, Sent You His king - dom to pro - claim, His ho - ly will to do.
3 Straight - way and stead - fast un - til death You then o - beyed His call Free - ly as Son of Man to serve And give Your life for all.
4 Bap - tize us with Your Spir - it, Lord, Your cross on us be signed, That, like - wise in God's ser - vice we May per - fect free - dom find.

As Jesus began His ministry, He was baptized to "fulfill all righteousness."
In the Word-drenched water of Holy Baptism, we share in Christ's
righteousness and receive the Holy Spirit.

Text: F. Bland Tucker, 1895–1984, alt.
Tune: *The CL Psalmes of David,* Edinburgh, 1635; setting: *The English Hymnal,* 1906

CAITHNESS
CM

Matt. 3:13–17; Acts 10:38; Mark 10:45

816   To Jordan's River Came Our Lord

1 To Jor - dan's riv - er came our Lord, The
2 The Sav - ior came to be bap - tized— The
3 As Je - sus in the Jor - dan stood And
4 Then from God's throne with thun - d'rous sound Came

Christ, whom heav'n-ly hosts a - dored, The God from God, the
Son of God in flesh dis-guised— To stand be - neath the
John bap - tized the Lamb of God, The Ho - ly Spir - it,
God's own voice with words pro-found: "This is My Son," was

Light from Light, The Lord of glo - ry, pow'r, and might.
Fa - ther's will And all His prom - is - es ful - fill.
heav'n-ly dove, De - scend - ed on Him from a - bove.
His de - cree, "The one I love, who pleas - es Me."

5 The Father's word, the Spirit's flight
Anointed Christ in glorious sight
As God's own choice, from Adam's fall
To save the world and free us all.

6 Now rise, faint hearts: be resolute!
This man is Christ, our substitute!
He was baptized in Jordan's stream,
Proclaimed Redeemer, Lord supreme.

Text: James P. Tiefel, b. 1949
Tune: *Musicalisch Hand-Buch der Geistlichen Melodien,* Hamburg, 1690, alt.; setting: William H. Monk, 1823–89
Text: © 1993 James P. Tiefel
Music: Public domain

WINCHESTER NEW
LM

Matt. 3:13–17; Acts 10:38

Come, Join in Cana's Feast

817

1 Come, join in Cana's feast Where Christ is hon-ored guest. He wel-comes all who come to taste The wine His hands have blessed.

2 The old wine now is gone From jars that stand a-part. No long-er can it sat-is-fy The yearn-ing, thirst-ing heart.

3 But Christ, the Word made flesh, Bids wa-ter turn to wine. He fills our emp-ty cups a-gain With grace and truth di-vine.

4 Come, friends, and share the feast; Here guest and host; For us, the cru-ci-fied.

5 For now He lives and reigns Through all e-ter-ni-ty With Fa-ther, Spir-it, three in one, The glo-rious Trin-i-ty.

As Jesus revealed His glory in the miraculous sign at Cana, so does He now
give Himself in the miraculous sign of His body and blood.

Text: Herman G. Stuempfle, Jr., b. 1923
Tune: *Harmonischer Lieder-Schatz*, Frankfurt, 1738; adapt. William H. Havergal, 1793–1870. Setting: composite

FRANCONIA
SM

John 2:1–11; Rev. 19:7–9; 1 Cor. 11:23–26

818   Jesus on the Mountain Peak

1 Jesus on the mountain peak / Stands alone in
2 Trembling at His feet we saw / Moses and E-
3 Swift the cloud of glory came: / God proclaiming
4 This is God's beloved Son! / Law and prophets

glory blazing; / Let us, if we dare to speak,
lijah speaking. / All the prophets and the law
in its thunder / Jesus as the Son by name!
sing before Him, / First and last and only One.

Join the saints and angels praising.
Shout through them their joyful greeting.
Nations, cry aloud in wonder:
All creation shall adore Him!

Alleluia!

This transfiguration text by contemporary English poet Brian Wren is here united with a new tune written especially for this supplement by Theodore Beck, long-time professor at Concordia University, Seward, Nebraska.

Text: Brian Wren, b. 1936
Music: Theodore A. Beck, b. 1929

SEWARD
78 78 4

Matt. 17:1–8; 2 Peter 1:16–19

Alleluia, Song of Gladness 819

1 Al - le - lu - ia, song of glad - ness, Voice of joy that
2 Al - le - lu - ia, thou re - sound - est, True Je - ru - sa -
3 Al - le - lu - ia can - not al - ways Be our song while
4 There - fore in our hymns we pray Thee, Grant us, bless - ed

can - not die; Al - le - lu - ia is the an - them
lem and free; Al - le - lu - ia, joy - ful moth - er,
here be - low; Al - le - lu - ia, our trans - gres - sions
Trin - i - ty, At the last to keep Thine Eas - ter

Ev - er raised by choirs on high; In the house of
All thy chil - dren sing with thee, But by Bab - y -
Make us for a while for - go; For the sol - emn
With Thy faith - ful saints on high; There to Thee for -

God a - bid - ing Thus they sing e - ter - nal - ly.
lon's sad wa - ters Mourn - ing ex - iles now are we.
time is com - ing When our tears for sin must flow.
ev - er sing - ing Al - le - lu - ia joy - ful - ly.

*The arrival of Lent marks our entrance into a 40-day exile of repentance as we
meditate on our Lord's Passion. This Transfiguration Sunday text "buries" the use of
alleluia during the Lenten season until our alleluias resound again on Easter.*

Text: Latin hymn, 11th cent.; tr. John M. Neale, 1818–66, alt.
Music: John Goss, 1800–80

LAUDA ANIMA (PRAISE, MY SOUL)
87 87 87

Ps. 137:1–6

820 Your Heart, O God, Is Grieved

Cantor

1 O God, Father in heav - en, have mer - cy up - on us.
2 O Son of God, Redeemer of the world, have mer - cy up - on us.
3 O God, Holy Spir - it, have mer - cy up - on us.

Congregation

Your heart, O God, is grieved, we know, By ev - 'ry e - vil,
Your arms ex - tend, O Christ, to save From sting of death and
O lav - ish Giv - er, come to aid The fee - ble child Your

ev - 'ry woe; Up - on Your cross - for -
grasp of grave; Your scars be - fore the
grace has made. Now make us grow and

sak - en Son Our death is laid, and peace is won.
Fa - ther move His heart to mer - cy at such love.
help us pray; Bring joy and com - fort; come to stay.

Text: Jiří Tranovský, 1591–1637; tr. Jaroslav J. Vajda, b. 1919
Tune: *Pisne duchovni*, Levoca, 1636; setting: Michael Kútsky, 1828–99

ZNÁME TO, PANE BOŽE NÁŠ
Irregular

Text: © 1970 Jaroslav J. Vajda
Music: Public domain

Is. 53:3–6; 1 Cor. 15:55–58

Deep Were His Wounds

821

1 Deep were His wounds, and red, On cru-el Cal-va-ry,
2 He suf-fered shame and scorn, And wretch-ed, dire dis-grace;
3 His life, His all, He gave When He was cru-ci-fied;

As on the cross He bled In bit-ter ag-o-ny.
For-sak-en and for-lorn, He hung there in our place.
Our bur-dened souls to save, What fear-ful death He died!

But they, whom sin has wound-ed sore,
But all who would from sin be free
But each of us, though dead in sin,

Find heal-ing in the wounds He bore.
Look to His cross for vic-to-ry.
Through Him e-ter-nal life may win.

Text: William Johnson, 1906–91
Music: Leland B. Sateren, b. 1913

MARLEE
66 66 88

Text and music: © 1958 *Service Book and Hymnal*, admin. Augsburg Fortress

1 Peter 2:24; Eph. 2:4–5; Heb. 12:1–3; Is. 53:7

822

The Lamb

1 The Lamb, the Lamb, O Fa - ther, where's the sac - ri - fice? Faith
2 The Lamb, the Lamb, One per - fect fi - nal of - fer - ing. The
3 The Lamb, the Lamb, As way - ward sheep their shep - herd kill So
4 He sighs, He dies, He takes my sin and wretch - ed - ness. He
5 He rose, He rose, My heart with thanks now o - ver - flows. His

sees, be - lieves God will pro - vide the Lamb of price!
Lamb, the Lamb, Let earth join heav'n His praise to sing.
still, His will On our be - half the Law to fill.
lives, for - gives, He gives me His own righ - teous - ness.
song pro - long 'Til ev - 'ry heart to Him be - long.

Refrain

Wor - thy is the Lamb whose death makes me His

own! The Lamb is reign - ing on His throne!

Abraham's willingness to sacrifice his only son and heir, Isaac, foreshadowed God the Father's willing provision of His Son, the true Lamb sacrificed for all sin.

Text: Gerald P. Coleman, b. 1953
Music: Gerald P. Coleman, b. 1953

WINTER
48 48 and Refrain

Rev. 5:12–13; Gen. 22:7–8; 1 Peter 2:24–25

Cross of Jesus, Cross of Sorrow 823

1 Cross of Je - sus, cross of sor - row,
2 Here the King of all the a - ges,
3 O mys - ter - ious con - de - scend - ing!
4 Cross of Je - sus, cross of sor - row,

Where the blood of Christ was shed,
Throned in light ere worlds could be,
O a - ban - don - ment sub - lime!
Where the blood of Christ was shed,

Per - fect man on thee did suf - fer,
Robed in mor - tal flesh is dy - ing,
Ver - y God Him - self is bear - ing
Per - fect man on thee did suf - fer,

Per - fect God on thee has bled!
Cru - ci - fied by sin for me.
All the suf - fer - ings of time!
Per - fect God on thee has bled!

Text: William J. Sparrow-Simpson, 1860–1952
Music: John Stainer, 1840–1901

Text and music: Public domain

CROSS OF JESUS
87 87

Col. 1:19–20; Is. 53:10–11; Phil. 2:5–11; 1 Cor. 1:18

824   In Silent Pain the Eternal Son

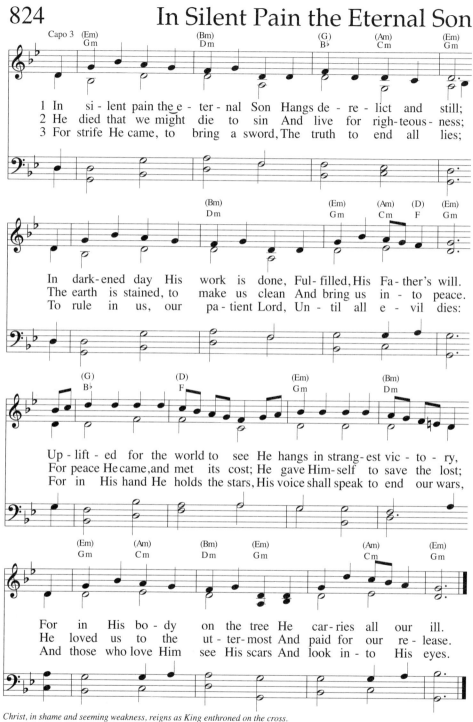

1 In silent pain the eternal Son Hangs derelict and still;
2 He died that we might die to sin And live for righteousness;
3 For strife He came, to bring a sword, The truth to end all lies;

In darkened day His work is done, Fulfilled, His Father's will.
The earth is stained, to make us clean And bring us into peace.
To rule in us, our patient Lord, Until all evil dies:

Uplifted for the world to see He hangs in strangest victory,
For peace He came, and met its cost; He gave Himself to save the lost;
For in His hand He holds the stars, His voice shall speak to end our wars,

For in His body on the tree He carries all our ill.
He loved us to the uttermost And paid for our release.
And those who love Him see His scars And look into His eyes.

Christ, in shame and seeming weakness, reigns as King enthroned on the cross.
By His death, Jesus gains the victory over sin on our behalf, fully paying for all
human iniquity. This text and tune are from the Iona Community of Scotland.

Text: Christopher Idle, b. 1938
Tune: John Bell, b. 1949; setting: Henry V. Gerike, b. 1948, and Joseph Herl, b. 1959

Text: © 1992 Hope Publishing Co.
Tune: © GIA Publications, Inc.   Setting: © 1998 Concordia Publishing House

REALITY
86 86 88 86

Matt. 10:34–39; 27:45–54; 1 Peter 2:24

When Israel Was in Egypt's Land 825

1 When Is - rael was in E - gypt's land,
2 The Lord told Mo - ses what to do,
3 The pillar of cloud shall clear the way,
4 As Is - rael stood by the wa - ter - side,
5 When they had reached the oth - er shore,
6 Oh, let us all from bond - age flee,

Let My peo-ple go;

Op- pressed so hard they could not stand,
To lead the children of Is - rael through,
A fire by night, a shade by day,
At God's com-mand it did di - vide,
They sang the song of tri - umph o'er,
And let us all in Christ be free,

Let My peo-ple go.

Refrain

Go down, Mo - ses, way down in E-gypt's land,

Tell old Pha - raoh: Let My peo-ple go.

Text: African American spiritual
Tune: African American spiritual; setting: John W. Work, 1871–1925

TUBMAN
85 85 and refrain

Text and music: Public domain

Ex. 5:1–2; 14–15; 1 Cor. 10:1–13

No Tramp of Soldiers' Marching Feet

826

1 No tramp of sol - diers' march - ing feet With
2 And yet He comes. The chil - dren cheer; With
3 What fad - ing flow'rs His road a - dorn; The
4 Now He who bore for mor - tals' sake The

ban - ners and with drums, No sound of mu - sic's
palms His path is strown. With ev - 'ry step the
palms, how soon laid down! No bloom or leaf but
cross and all its pains And chose a ser - vant's

mar - tial beat— "The King of glo - ry comes!" To
cross draws near— The King of glo - ry's throne. A -
on - ly thorn The King of glo - ry's crown. The
form to take, The King of glo - ry reigns. Ho -

greet what pomp of king - ly pride No
stride a colt He pass - es by As
sol - diers mock, the rab - ble cries, The
san - na to the Sav - ior's name Till

This hymn may be sung to the tune ELLACOMBE.

Text: Timothy Dudley-Smith, b. 1926
Music: English folk tune; adapt. and harm. Ralph Vaughan Williams, 1872–1958

Text: © 1984 Hope Publishing Co.
Music: Public domain

KINGSFOLD
CM D

Luke 19:37–38; Matt. 21:5–9; John 19:14–18

bells	in	tri - umph	ring,	No	cit - y	gates	swing
loud	ho -	san - nas	ring,	Or	else the	ver -	y
streets with	tu - mult	ring,	As	Pi - late	to	the
heav -	en's	raft - ers	ring,	And	all	the	ran - somed

o - pen wide: "Be - hold, be - hold your King!"
stones would cry "Be - hold, be - hold your King!"
mob re - plies, "Be - hold, be - hold your King!"
host pro - claim "Be - hold, be - hold your King!"

Jesus, Remember Me 827

Capo 1 (D) (Em/D) (A) (D)
E♭ Fm/E♭ B♭ E♭

Je-sus, re-mem-ber me when You come in - to Your King-dom.

(Bm) (Em/G) (A) (D)
Cm Fm/A♭ B♭ E♭

Je-sus, re-mem-ber me when You come in - to Your King-dom.

Text: Luke 23:42
Music: Jacques Berthier, 1923–94

REMEMBER ME
Irregular

Luke 23:42

828   Christ Has Arisen, Alleluia

1 Christ has a - ris - en, al - le - lu - ia.
2 For three long days the grave did its worst
3 The an - gel said to them, "Do not fear.
4 "Go spread the news: He's not in the grave.
5 Christ has a - ris - en; He sets us free.

Re - joice and praise Him, al - le - lu - ia.
Un - til its strength by God was dis - persed.
You look for Je - sus who is not here.
He has a - ris - en this world to save.
Al - le - lu - ia, to Him prais - es be.

For our Re - deem - er burst from the tomb,
He who gives life did death un - der - go.
See for your - selves the tomb is all bare.
Je - sus' re - deem - ing la - bors are done.
Je - sus is liv - ing! Let us all sing;

E - ven from death, dis - pel - ling its gloom.
And in its con - quest His might did show.
On - ly the grave cloths are ly - ing there."
E - ven the bat - tle with sin is won."
He reigns tri - um - phant, heav - en - ly king.

The Church is growing rapidly today in places such as Tanzania, a
country which boasts the largest number of Lutherans in Africa. This
Easter hymn unites us in a common song of praise to our risen Savior.

Text: Bernard Kyamanywa, b. 1938; tr. Howard S. Olson, b. 1922
Music: Traditional Tanzanian

MFURAHINI HALELUYA
99 99 and refrain

Mark 16:6–7; 1 Cor. 15:5–57

Refrain

Let us sing praise to Him with end - less joy.

Death's fear - ful sting He has come to de - stroy.

Our sin for - giv - ing, al - le - lu - ia!

Je - sus is liv - ing, al - le - lu - ia!

829 All the Earth with Joy Is Sounding

1 All the earth with joy is sound - ing: Christ has ris - en
2 Christ, the de - vil's might un - wind - ing, Leaves be - hind His
3 Je - sus, au - thor of sal - va - tion, Shared in our hu -
4 Praise the Lord, His reign com - menc - es, Reign of life and

from the dead! He, the great - er Jo - nah, bound - ing From the
bor - rowed tomb. Strong - er He, the strong man bind - ing, Takes, dis -
man - i - ty; Crowned with ra - diant ex - al - ta - tion, Now He
lib - er - ty— Pas - chal Lamb, for our of - fens - es, Slain and

grave, His three - day bed, Wins the prize: Death's de -
arms his house of doom; In the rout Cast - ing
shares His vic - to - ry! From His face Shines the
raised to set us free! Ev - er - more Bow be -

mise— Songs of tri - umph fill the skies.
out Pow'rs of dark - ness, sin, and doubt.
grace Meant for all our fall - en race.
fore Christ, the Lord of Life a - dore!

Jesus gave the people of His day "the sign of Jonah," pointing them to the day
when He would rise from the grave. By His death and resurrection, Christ
indeed plundered the devil's (the strong man's) house and won the victory.

Text: Stephen P. Starke, b. 1955
Music: Herbert Howells, 1892–1983

MICHAEL
87 87 33 7

Matt. 12:39–41; Mark 3:27; Heb. 2:7–15; 12:2

Our Paschal Lamb, That Sets Us Free 830

1 Our Pas-chal Lamb, that sets us free, Is sac-ri-ficed. Oh,
2 Let all our lives now cel-e-brate The feast; let mal-ice
3 Let all our deeds, u-nan-i-mous, Con-fess Him as our

keep The feast of free-dom gal-lant-ly; Let al-le-lu-ias
die. Let love grow strong a-new, and great, Let truth stamp out the
Lord Who by the Spir-it lives in us, The Fa-ther's liv-ing

Refrain

leap:
lie. Al-le-lu-ia! Al-le-lu-ia! Al-le-lu-ia! A-
Word.

gain Sing al-le-lu-ia, cry a-loud: Al-le-lu-ia! A-men!

This Easter text by Martin Franzmann is published in a hymnal here for the first time with the tune written for it more than 20 years ago by Walter Pelz, now professor emeritus at Bethany College, Lindsborg, Kansas.

Text: Martin H. Franzmann, 1907–76
Music: Walter L. Pelz, b. 1926

REGION THREE
CM and refrain

Text and music: © 1974 Augsburg Publishing House

1 Cor. 5:7–8

These Things
Did Thomas Count as Real

831

1 These things did Thom - as count as real: The
2 The vi - sion of his skep - tic mind Was
3 His rea - soned cer - tain - ties de - nied That
4 May we, O God, by grace be - lieve And

warmth of blood, the chill of steel, The grain of wood, the
keen e - nough to make him blind To an - y un - ex -
one could live when one had died, Un - til his fin - gers
thus the ris - en Christ re - ceive, Whose raw im-print - ed

heft of stone, The last frail twitch of flesh and bone.
pect - ed act Too large for his small world of fact.
read like braille The mark - ings of the spear and nail.
palms reached out And beck - oned Thom-as from his doubt.

A hallmark of the texts of Thomas Troeger, a modern American hymnwriter, is his use of stark, vivid imagery. Jesus' postresurrection appearance to the apostle Thomas removed his doubt and rekindled his faith. This hymn may also be sung to ERHALT UNS, HERR.

Text: Thomas H. Troeger, b. 1945
Music: English folk tune; setting: Henry V. Gerike, b. 1948
Text: © 1984 Oxford University Press
Tune: Public domain   Setting: © 1998 Concordia Publishing House

TRUTH FROM ABOVE
LM

John 20:19–31

Long Before the World Is Waking

832

1 Long be - fore the world is wak - ing, Morn - ing mist on
2 So they cast, and all their heav - ing Can - not haul their
3 Char - coal em - bers bright - ly burn - ing, Bread and fish up -
4 Christ is ris - en! Grief and sigh - ing, Sins and sor - rows,
5 Morn - ing breaks, and Je - sus meets us, Feeds and com - forts,

Gal - i - lee, From the shore, as dawn is break - ing,
catch a - board; John in won - der turns, per - ceiv - ing,
on them laid: Je - sus stands at day's re - turn - ing,
fall be - hind; Fear and fail - ure, doubt, de - ny - ing,
par - dons still; As His faith - ful friends He greets us,

Je - sus calls a - cross the sea; Hails the boat of
Cries a - loud, "It is the Lord!" Pe - ter waits for
In His ris - en life ar - rayed; As of old His
Full and free for - give-ness find. All the soul's dark
Part - ners of His work and will. All our days, on

wea - ry men, Bids them cast their net a - gain.
noth - ing more, Plung - es in to swim a - shore.
friends to greet, "Here is break - fast; come and eat."
night is past, Morn - ing breaks in joy at last.
ev - 'ry shore, Christ is ours for ev - er - more!

Text: Timothy Dudley-Smith, b. 1926
Tune: *Geistreiches Gesangbuch*, Darmstadt, 1698; setting: *Hymns Ancient and Modern*, 1861
Text: © 1984 Hope Publishing Co.
Music: Public domain

ALL SAINTS (ZEUCH MICH)
87 87 77

John 21:1–17

833 Christ Is Risen, Christ Is Living

1 Christ is ris - en, Christ is liv - ing, Dry your tears, be un - a - fraid!
1 ¡Cris - to vi - ve, fue-ra_el llan-to, los la - men-tos y_el pe - sar!
2 If the Lord had nev - er ris - en, We'd have noth - ing to be - lieve;
2 Que si Cris-to no vi - vie-ra va - na fue - ra nues-tra fe;

Death and dark-ness could not hold Him, Nor the tomb in which He lay.
Ni la muer-te ni_el se - pul-cro lo_han po - di - do su - je - tar.
But His prom-ise can be trust-ed: "You will live, be-cause I live."
Mas se cum-ple su pro-me - sa: "Por-que vi - vo, vi - vi-réis."

Do not look a-mong the dead for One who lives for - ev - er - more;
No bus-quéis en - tre los muer-tos al que siem-pre_ha de vi - vir,
As we share the death of Ad-am, So in Christ we live a - gain;
Si_en A - dán en - tró la muer-te, por Je - sús la vi - da_en - tró;

Tell the world that Christ is ris - en, Make it known He goes be - fore.
¡Cris - to vi - ve, es - tas nue-vas por do-quier de-jad o - ir.
Death has lost its sting and ter - ror, Christ the Lord has come to reign.
No te - máis, el triun-fo_es vues-tro: ¡El Se - ñor re - su - ci - tó!

This Easter hymn from Argentina expresses both Christ's triumph over death and our living hope in Him. The text, by a South American pastor and poet, is joined to this tune by an internationally known composer of liturgical music.

Text: Nicholas Martinez, 1917–72; tr. Fred Kaan, b. 1929
Tune: Pablo D. Sosa, b. 1933; setting: Richard J. Heschke, b. 1939

CENTRAL (ARGENTINA)
87 87 D

1 Cor. 15:12–23; 55–57; John 14:19; Rom. 6:3–5

3 Death has lost its old dominion,
    Let the world rejoice and shout!
Christ, the first-born of the living,
    Gives us life and leads us out.
Let us thank our God, who causes
    Hope to spring up from the ground.
Christ is risen, Christ is giving
    Life eternal, life profound.

3 *Si es verdad que de la muerte*
    El pecado es aguijón,
No temáis pues Jesucristo
    Nos da vida y salvación.
Gracias demos al Dios Padre
    Que nos da seguridad,
Que quien cree en Jesucristo
    Vive por la eternidad.

Now Is Eternal Life 834

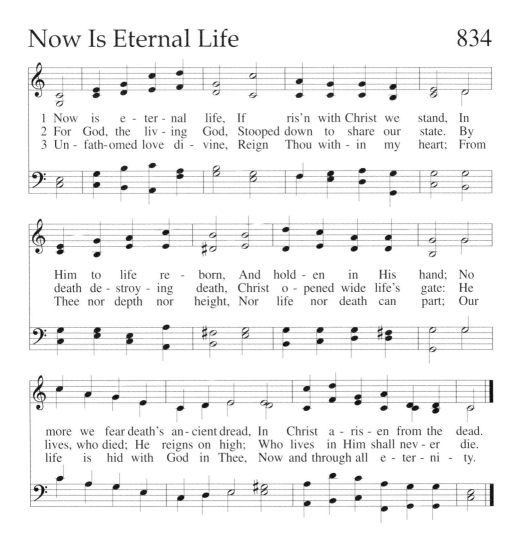

1 Now is e-ter-nal life, If ris'n with Christ we stand, In
2 For God, the liv-ing God, Stooped down to share our state. By
3 Un-fath-omed love di-vine, Reign Thou with-in my heart; From

Him to life re-born, And hold-en in His hand; No
death de-stroy-ing death, Christ o-pened wide life's gate: He
Thee nor depth nor height, Nor life nor death can part; Our

more we fear death's an-cient dread, In Christ a-ris-en from the dead.
lives, who died; He reigns on high; Who lives in Him shall nev-er die.
life is hid with God in Thee, Now and through all e-ter-ni-ty.

Text: George W. Briggs, 1875–1959, alt.
Music: Charles Steggall, 1826–1905

CHRISTCHURCH
66 66 88

Col. 3:1–4; John 11:25–26; 1 Cor. 15:54–57

835   Holy Spirit, Gift of God

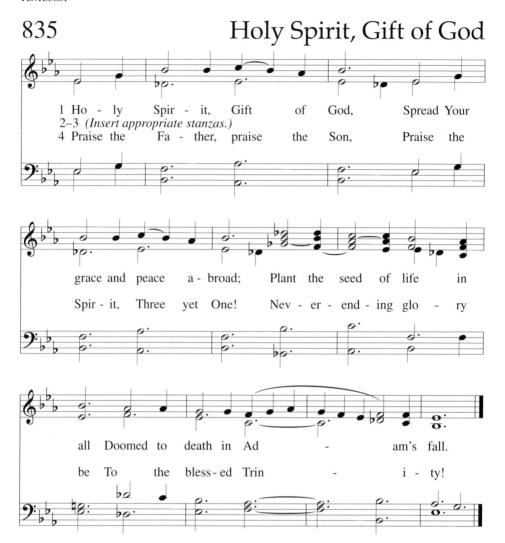

1 Ho - ly Spir - it, Gift of God, Spread Your
2–3 *(Insert appropriate stanzas.)*
4 Praise the Fa - ther, praise the Son, Praise the

grace and peace a - broad; Plant the seed of life in
Spir - it, Three yet One! Nev - er - end - ing glo - ry

all Doomed to death in Ad - am's fall.
be To the bless - ed Trin - i - ty!

Reflecting the declarations of the Third Article of the Apostles' Creed, the
various stanzas of this hymn may be inserted between the first and last stanzas
in order to emphasize different aspects of the work of the Holy Spirit.

Text: Jaroslov J. Vajda, b. 1919
Music: Ralph Vaughan Williams, 1872–1958; adapt. E. Harold Greer, 1886–1957

THE CALL
77 77

1 Cor. 12:3; Rom. 8:14–17; 1 Peter 3:18–21

I Believe in the Holy Spirit

5 Long before I knew Your name,
In my heart You lit Your flame;
By the Water and the Word
My adoption was conferred.

6 Best Gift God the Father gives,
Who receives It dies and lives.
Ask—It will not be refused!
Pray—how is It to be used?

The Holy Christian Church, the Communion of Saints

7 One is nevermore alone
Who is kin to God's dear Son;
All are joined in unity
In God's timeless family.

8 New in outlook, new in hope,
Heightened vision, broadened scope;
In them glows a love divine,
Through them Jesus' virtues shine.

The Forgiveness of Sins

9 Melter of the hardened heart,
Show all who have grown apart
What it means to be forgiv'n
And to be an heir of heav'n.

10 Ever since the Spirit came,
We are freed from guilt and shame;
Spirit-led and Spirit-fed,
Free to follow Christ our Head.

The Resurrection of the Body

11 Show the love, the cross, the grave—
Show all Christ has done to save;
Show the resurrected Word;
Cry in us: "My God! My Lord!"

12 Christ who lived for us and died,
By the Spirit was revived;
By that Spirit we shall too
Rise from death to life anew

And the Life Everlasting

13 From the Spirit comes the breath—
Breath that will not end in death,
But revives to breathe the air
Of a bliss beyond compare.

14 What creation could have been
Unstained by the curse of sin,
We shall know in fullest bloom
In our promised perfect home.

836

O Trinity, O Trinity

1 O Trin - i - ty, O Trin - i - ty, the un - cre - at - ed
2 O Maj - es - ty, O Maj - es - ty, Cre - a - tor of our
3 O Vir - gin - born, O Vir - gin - born, of hu - man - kind the
4 O Wind of God, O Wind of God, in - vig - or - ate the

One; O U - ni - ty, O U - ni - ty, of
race; O Mys - ter - y, O Mys - ter - y, we
least; O Vic - tim torn, O Vic - tim torn, both
dead; O Fire of God, O Fire of God, Your

Fa - ther, Spir - it, Son: You are with - out be -
can - not see Your face: Your jus - tice is un -
spot - less lamb and priest: You died and rose vic -
burn - ing ra - diance spread: Your fruit our lives re -

gin - ning, Your life is nev - er end - ing;
swerv - ing, Your love is o - ver - pow - 'ring;
to - rious, You reign a - bove all - glo - rious;
new - ing, Your gifts the Church trans - form - ing;

With direct language, this hymn distinguishes the unique work of
each Person of the Godhead—Father, Son, and Holy Spirit—the
great mystery of the Trinity in Unity and the Unity in Trinity.

Text: Michael Saward, b. 1932
Music: Kenneth W. Coates, b. 1917

TRINITY
86 86 77 88

Text: © 1982 Hope Publishing Co.
Music: © Kenneth W. Coates

2 Cor. 4:6–7; Ex. 33:20–23; John 1:29–30; Acts 2:1–4

Refrain

And though our tongues are earth - bound clay,

Light them with flam - ing fire to - day.

5 O Trinity, O Trinity,
   The uncreated One
  O Unity, O Unity
   Of Father, Spirit, Son:
  You are without beginning,
   Your life is never ending; *Refrain*

Now Greet the Swiftly Changing Year

837

1 Now greet the swift - ly chang - ing year With
2 Re - mem - ber now the Son of God And
3 This Je - sus came to end sin's war; This
4 His love a - bun - dant far ex - ceeds The
5 With Him as Lord to lead our way In

joy and pen - i - tence sin - cere. Re - joice! Re-joice! With
how He shed His in - fant blood. Re - joice! Re-joice! With
Name of names for us He bore. Re - joice! Re-joice! With
vol - ume of a whole year's needs. Re - joice! Re-joice! With
want and in pros - per - i - ty, What need we fear in

thanks em - brace An - oth - er year of grace.
thanks em - brace An - oth - er year of grace.
thanks em - brace An - oth - er year of grace.
thanks em - brace An - oth - er year of grace.
earth or space In this new year of grace!

6 "All glory be to God on high,
And peace on earth!" the angels cry.
Rejoice! Rejoice! With thanks embrace
Another year of grace.

7 God, Father, Son, and Spirit, hear!
To all our pleas incline Your ear;
Upon our lives rich blessing trace
In this new year of grace.

Text: Slovak, 17th cent; tr. Jaroslav J. Vajda, b. 1919, alt.
Music: Alfred V. Fedak, b. 1953

Text: © 1969 Jaroslav J. Vajda
Music: © 1990 Selah Publishing Company

SIXTH NIGHT
88 86

Ps. 65:11; 107:8; Luke 2:21; Heb. 4:16

Oh, What Their Joy

838

1 Oh, what their joy and their glo - ry must be,
2 In new Je - ru - sa - lem joy shall be found,
3 We, where no trou - ble dis - trac - tion can bring,
4 Now let us wor - ship our Lord and our King,

Those end - less Sab - baths the bless - ed ones see!
Bless - ings of peace shall for - ev - er a - bound;
Safe - ly the an - thems of Zi - on shall sing;
Joy - ful - ly rais - ing our voic - es to sing:

Crowns for the val - iant, to wea - ry ones rest;
Wish and ful - fill - ment are not sev - ered there,
While for Your grace, Lord, their voic - es of praise
Praise to the Fa - ther, and praise to the Son,

God shall be all, and in all ev - er blest.
Nor the things prayed for come short of the prayer.
Your bless - ed peo - ple shall ev - er - more raise.
Praise to the Spir - it, to God, Three in One.

Text: Peter Abelard, 1079–1142; tr. John M. Neale, 1818–66, alt.
Tune: *Antiphoner*, Paris, 1681; setting: David Evans, 1874–1948

O QUANTA QUALIA
10 10 10 10

Rev. 7:10–17; 21:2–7

839 Sing with All the Saints in Glory

1 Sing with all the saints in glory, Sing the res - ur - rec - tion
2 Oh, what glo - ry, far ex - ceed - ing All that eye has yet per -
3 Life e - ter - nal! Heav'n re - joic - es: Je - sus lives who once was

song! Death and sor - row, earth's dark sto - ry,
ceived! Ho - liest hearts for a - ges plead - ing
dead. Shout with joy, O death - less voic - es!

To the for - mer days be - long. All a - round the
Nev - er that full joy con - ceived. God has prom - ised,
Child of God, lift up your head! Life e - ter - nal!

clouds are break - ing, Soon the storms of time shall cease;
Christ pre - pares it, There on high our wel - come waits.
Oh, what won - ders Crowd on faith; what joy un - known,

This new tune reflects well the vivid word pictures of this text.
Christians endure the trials of this life, confident of God's promise
of eternal life, for He has made us His saints in Christ Jesus.

Text: William J. Irons, 1812–83, alt.
Music: William B. Roberts, b. 1949

MISSISSIPPI
87 87 D

Rev. 7:9–17; 21:1–5; 1 Cor. 2:9; John 14:1–3

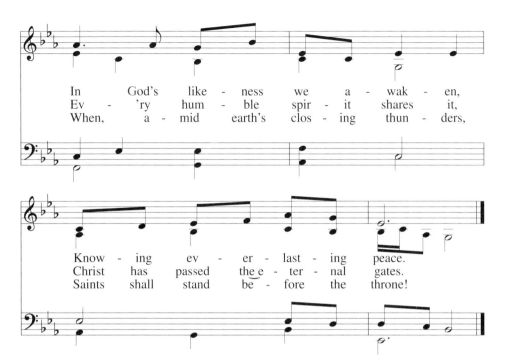

In God's like - ness we a - wak - en,
Ev - 'ry hum - ble spir - it shares it,
When, a - mid earth's clos - ing thun - ders,

Know - ing ev - er - last - ing peace.
Christ has passed the e - ter - nal gates.
Saints shall stand be - fore the throne!

840   Saints, See the Cloud of Witnesses

1 Saints, see the cloud of wit-ness-es sur-round us;
2 These saints of old re-ceived God's com-men-da-tion.
3 They call to us, "Your tim-id foot-steps length-en;
4 Come, let us fix our sight on Christ who suf-fered,

Their lives of faith en-cour-age and as-tound us.
They lived as pil-grim-heirs of His sal-va-tion.
Throw off sin's weight, your halt-ing weak-ness strength-en.
He faced the cross, His sin-less life He of-fered;

Hear how the Mas-ter praised their faith so
Through faith they con-quered flame and sword and
We kept the faith, we shed our blood, were
He scorned the shame, He died, our death en-

fer-vent: "Well done, My ser-vant!"
gal-lows, God's name to hal-low.
mar-tyred; Our lives we bar-tered."
dur-ing, Our hope se-cur-ing.

Text: Stephen P. Starke, b. 1955
Tune: Dale Wood, b. 1934; setting: Steven F. Wente, b. 1952

Text: © 1997 Stephen P. Starke.   Setting: © 1998 Concordia Publishing House
Tune: © 1974 Augsburg Publishing House

WOJTKIEWIECZ
11 11 11 5

Heb. 11:32–12:3; Matt. 25:21

5 Lord, give us faith
    to walk where You are sending,
On paths unmarked,
    eyes blind as to their ending;
Not knowing where we go,
    but that You lead us—
With grace precede us.

6 You, Jesus, You alone
    deserve all glory!
Our lives unfold,
    embraced within Your story;
Past, present, future—
    You the same forever,
To fail us never!

HOLY BAPTISM

This Is the Spirit's Entry Now 841

1 This is the Spir - it's en - try now: The
2 This mir - a - cle of life re - born Comes
3 Let wa - ter be the sa - cred sign That
4 Re - new - ing Spir - it, hear our praise For

wa - ter and the Word, The cross of Je - sus
from the Lord of breath; The per - fect Man from
we must die each day To rise a - gain by
Your bap - tis - mal pow'r That wash - es us through

on your brow, The seal both felt and heard.
life was torn; Our life comes through Christ's death.
His de - sign As fol - low'rs of His way.
all our days. Lord, cleanse a - gain this hour.

Text: Thomas E. Herbranson, b. 1933
Music: Leo Sowerby, 1895–1968

Text: © Thomas E. Herbranson.
Music: © 1964 Abingdon Press, admin. The Copyright Company

PERRY
CM

Eph. 5:25b–27; Titus 3:5–7; Rom. 6:3–9

842 See This Wonder in the Making

1 See this won-der in the mak-ing: God Him-
2 Mir - a - cle each time it hap-pens As the
3 Far more ten-der than a moth-er, Far more
4 Here we bring a child of na-ture; Home we

self this child is tak-ing As a lamb safe in His
door to heav-en o - pens And the Fa-ther beams, "Be-
car-ing than a fa-ther, God, in - to Your arms we
take a new-born crea-ture, Now God's pre-cious son or

keep-ing, His to be, a-wake or sleep-ing.
lov-ed, Heir of gifts a king would cov-et!"
place *him/her*, With Your love and peace em-brace *him/her*.
daugh-ter, Born a-gain by Word and wa-ter.

Text: Jaroslav J. Vajda, b. 1919
Music: Swedish folk tune, *Lofsånger och andeliga wisor*, 1873

Text: © 1984 Jaroslav J. Vajda
Music: Public domain

TRYGGARE KAN INGEN VARA
88 88 (Trochaic)

Matt. 3:16–17; Titus 3:3–6; Eph. 5:25b–26; Mark 10:16

Cradling Children in His Arm

843

Cra-dling chil-dren in His arm, Je - sus gave His bless - ing.

To our babes a wel-come warm He is yet ad-dress - ing.

Take them, Lord, give life a - new In the liv-ing wa - ters!

Keep them al - ways near to You As Your sons and daugh - ters!

Text: Nikolai F. S. Grundtvig, 1783–1872; tr. Johannes H. V. Knudsen, 1902–82
Tune: Johann Horn, 1490–1547; setting: Theodore A. Beck, b. 1929

GAUDEAMUS PARITER
76 76 D

Mark 10:13–16; Titus 3:4–7; John 4:13–14

844 God's Own Child, I Gladly Say It

1 God's own child, I glad-ly say it: I am bap-tized
2 Sin, dis-turb my soul no long-er: I am bap-tized
3 Sa-tan, hear this proc-la-ma-tion: I am bap-tized
4 Death, you can-not end my glad-ness: I am bap-tized

in - to Christ! He, be-cause I could not pay it,
in - to Christ! I have com-fort e-ven strong-er:
in - to Christ! Drop your ug-ly ac-cu-sa-tion,
in - to Christ! When I die, I leave all sad-ness

Gave my full re-demp-tion price. Do I need earth's
Je - sus' cleans-ing sac-ri-fice. Should a guilt-y
I am not so soon en-ticed. Now that to the
To in-her-it par-a-dise! Though I lie in

trea - sures man-y? I have one worth
con - science seize me Since my Bap-tism
font I've trav-eled, All your might has
dust and ash-es Faith's as-sur-ance

*Both the joy of living as baptized sons and daughters in Christ and the daily
significance of remembering our Baptism are portrayed in this hymn. The
tune also reflects the exuberant joy of all who are baptized into Christ Jesus.*

Text: Erdmann Neumeister, 1671–1756; tr. Robert E. Voelker, b. 1957
Tune: Johann Caspar Bachofen, 1697–1755; setting: Joseph Herl, b. 1959

BACHOFEN
87 87 88 77

Text: © 1991 Robert E. Voelker
Tune: Public domain.   Setting: © 1998 Concordia Publishing House

Rom. 6:1–10; 1 Peter 3:18–22; Titus 3:4–7

more   than   an - y   That   brought   me   sal -
did   re - lease   me   In   a   dear   for -
come   un - rav - eled,   And,   a - gainst   your
bright - ly flash - es: Bap - tism   has   the

va - tion   free   Last - ing   to   e - ter - ni - ty!
giv - ing   flood,   Sprink - ling   me   with   Je - sus' blood?
ty - ran - ny,   God,   my   Lord,   u - nites   with me!
strength di - vine   To   make   life   im - mor - tal   mine.

5 There is nothing worth comparing
   To this lifelong comfort sure!
   Open-eyed my grave is staring:
   Even there I'll sleep secure.

Though my flesh awaits its raising,
   Still my soul continues praising:
   I am baptized into Christ;
   I'm a child of paradise!

You Have Put on Christ

845

You   have   put on   Christ,   In   Him   you have been   bap - tized.

You   have put on   Christ,   Al - le   -   lu - ia!

May be sung as a two- or three-part canon.

Text: Gal. 3:27; International Committee on English in the Liturgy (ICEL)
Music: Howard Hughes, b. 1930

BAPTIZED IN CHRIST
Irregular

Gal. 3:27

846   We Know that Christ Is Raised

1 We know that Christ is raised and dies no more.
2 We share by wa - ter in His sav - ing death.
3 The Fa - ther's splen - dor clothes the Son with life.

Em - braced by death, He broke its fear - ful hold;
Re - born, we share with Him an Eas - ter life
The Spir - it's pow - er shakes the Church of God.

And our de - spair He turned to blaz - ing joy.
As liv - ing mem - bers of a liv - ing Christ.
Bap - tized, we live with God the Three in One.

Al - le - lu - ia! Al - le - lu - ia!

Text: John B. Geyer, b. 1932, alt.
Music: Charles V. Stanford, 1852–1924

Text: © John B. Geyer
Music: Public domain

ENGELBERG
10 10 10 4

Rom. 6:3–11; John 3:1–6

In All Our Grief

847

1 In all our grief and fear we turn to You.
2 Help us to put a - side the an - gry word,
3 You did not e - ven spare Your on - ly Son.
4 God, when we suf - fer all that we can bear,

O God, You know all that we think or do,
The clench - ing fist, the wish and will to hurt.
He lived our griefs and bore all e - vil done,
Then let us know that You in truth are near

You know the pain we put each oth - er through.
Teach us the way in which love best is served.
But through His cross, re - demp - tion has been won.
And will not leave us lost in all our fear.

Refrain

Lord, have mer - cy, Christ, have mer - cy, Lord, grant us peace.

Text: Sylvia G. Dunstan, 1955–93
Music: Charles R. Anders, b. 1929
Text: © 1991 GIA Publications, Inc.
Music: © 1978 *Lutheran Book of Worship*

FREDERICKTOWN
10 10 10 and refrain

Eph. 4:25–32; Is. 53:4–6

848

Now the Silence

Now the si - lence Now the peace Now the emp - ty hands up-lift - ed

Now the kneel - ing Now the plea Now the Fa - ther's arms in wel-come

Now the hear - ing Now the pow'r Now the ves - sel brimmed for pour - ing

Now the Bod - y Now the Blood Now the joy - ful cel - e - bra - tion

Now the wed - ding Now the songs Now the heart for - giv - en leap - ing

Weaving together worship images from the Divine Service—confession and absolution, Word and Sacrament—this hymn recalls the truth that now is the hour of grace, today is the day of salvation.

Text: Jaroslav J. Vajda, b. 1919
Music: Carl F. Schalk, b. 1929

NOW
PM

Rev. 19:7–10; 22:1–5; Luke 15:20–24

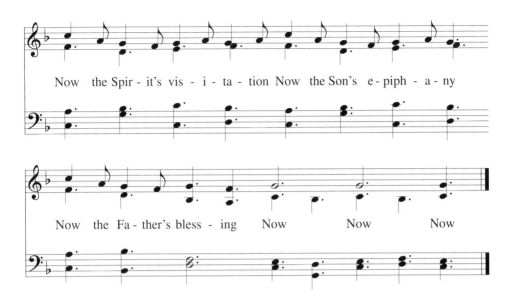

Now the Spir - it's vis - i - ta - tion Now the Son's e - piph - a - ny

Now the Fa - ther's bless - ing Now Now Now

849 Thee We Adore, O Hidden Savior

1 Thee we a - dore, O hid - den Sav - ior, Thee,
2 In this me - mo - rial of Thy death, O Lord,
3 Thou, like the pel - i - can to feed her brood,
4 Foun - tain of good - ness, Je - sus, Lord and God:
5 O Christ, whom now be - neath a veil we see:

Who in Thy Sac - ra - ment art pleased to be;
Thy bod - y and Thy blood Thou here af - ford:
Pierce Thy - self, giv - ing us Thy liv - ing food;
Cleanse us, un - clean, with Thy most cleans - ing blood;
May what we thirst for soon our por - tion be,

Both flesh and spir - it in Thy pres - ence fail,
Oh, may our souls for - ev - er feed on Thee,
Thy blood, O Lord, one drop has pow'r to win
In - crease our faith and love, that we may know
To gaze on Thee un - veiled, and see Thy face,

Yet here Thy pres - ence we de - vout - ly hail.
And Thou, O Christ, for - ev - er pre - cious be.
For - give - ness for our world and all its sin.
The hope and peace which from Thy pres - ence flow.
The vi - sion of Thy glo - ry, and Thy grace. A - men.

The third stanza of this hymn points to an ancient symbol of Christ's suffering and death: the pelican. In times of great need and hunger, the pelican mother unselfishly sacrifices herself so that her young brood might live.

Text: Thomas Aquinas, 1225–74; tr. James R. Woodford, 1820–85, alt.; sts. 2a and 3, Stephen P. Starke, b. 1955
Music: Mode V; *Processionale*, Paris, 1697; setting: Frederick F. Jackisch, b. 1922

Text: Sts. 1, 2b, 4–5 Public domain; sts. 2a, 3 © 1998 Concordia Publishing House
Tune: Public domain   Setting: © 1978 *Lutheran Book of Worship*

ADORO TE DEVOTE
10 10 10 10

Matt. 26:26–28; Ps. 36:7–9; 1 Cor. 11:24–25

What Is This Bread?

850

1 What is this bread? Christ's bod - y
2 What is this wine? The blood of
3 So who am I, That I should
4 Yet is God here? Oh, yes! By
5 Is this for me? I am for -

ris - en from the dead: This bread we break,
Je - sus shed for mine; The cup of grace
live and He should die Un - der the rod.
Word and prom - ise clear. In mouth and soul
giv - en and set free! I do be - lieve

This life we take, Was crushed to pay for our re -
Brings His em - brace Of life and love un - til I
My God, my God, Why have You not for - sak - en
He makes us whole— Christ, tru - ly pres - ent in this
That I re - ceive His ver - y bod - y and His

lease. Oh, taste and see— the Lord is peace.
sing! Oh, taste and see— the Lord is King.
me? Oh, taste and see— the Lord is free.
meal. Oh, taste and see— the Lord is real.
blood. Oh, taste and see— the Lord is good.

*This catechetical hymn was written for the weekly Eucharist at Messiah
Lutheran Church, Tucson, Arizona. It is based on the questions and answers on
Holy Communion in Luther's Small Catechism.*

Text: Frederic W. Baue, b. 1946
Music: Jean Neuhauser Baue, b. 1951

Text and music: © 1991 and 1998 Fred and Jean Baue   Setting: © 1998 Concordia Publishing House

PREPARATION
48 44 88

1 Cor. 11:23–29; Ps. 34:8; 1 Peter 2:2–3

851

Alleluia! Sing to Jesus

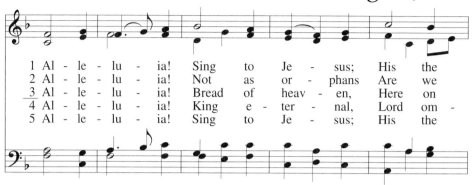

1 Al - le - lu - ia! Sing to Je - sus; His the
2 Al - le - lu - ia! Not as or - phans Are we
3 Al - le - lu - ia! Bread of heav - en, Here on
4 Al - le - lu - ia! King e - ter - nal, Lord om -
5 Al - le - lu - ia! Sing to Je - sus; His the

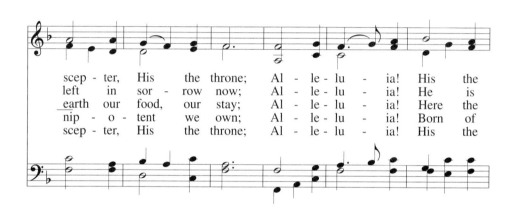

scep - ter, His the throne; Al - le - lu - ia! His the
left in sor - row now; Al - le - lu - ia! He is
earth our food, our stay; Al - le - lu - ia! Here the
nip - o - tent we own; Al - le - lu - ia! Born of
scep - ter, His the throne; Al - le - lu - ia! His the

tri - umph, His the vic - to - ry a - lone.
near us; Faith be - lieves, nor ques - tions how.
sin - ful Flee to You from day to day.
Mar - y, Earth Your foot - stool, heav'n Your throne.
tri - umph, His the vic - to - ry a - lone.

Though Christ has ascended to His Father's throne to intercede for us, we have His
promise that He remains with us in His Word and in His body and blood. Such a feast
hosted by the Friend of sinners impels our praises.

Text: William C. Dix, 1837–98, alt.
Music: Rowland H. Prichard, 1811–87

HYFRYDOL
87 87 D

Rev. 7:9–14; Acts 1:7–11; John 6:31–35; 14:18; Heb. 9:11–28

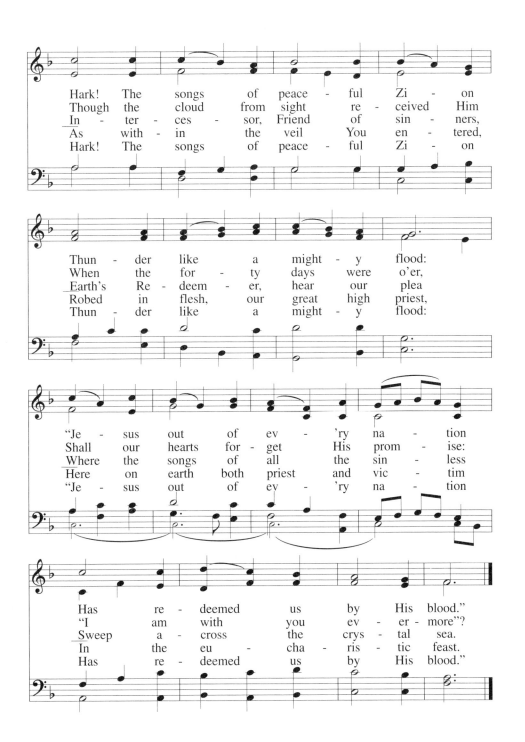

Hark! The songs of peace - ful Zi - on
Though the cloud from sight re - ceived Him
In - ter - ces - sor, Friend of sin - ners,
As with - in the veil You en - tered,
Hark! The songs of peace - ful Zi - on

Thun - der like a might - y flood:
When the for - ty days were o'er,
Earth's Re - deem - er, hear our plea
Robed in flesh, our great high priest,
Thun - der like a might - y flood:

"Je - sus out of ev - 'ry na - tion
Shall our hearts for - get His prom - ise:
Where the songs of all the sin - less
Here on earth both priest and vic - tim
"Je - sus out of ev - 'ry na - tion

Has re - deemed us by His blood."
"I am with you ev - er - more"?
Sweep a - cross the crys - tal sea.
In the eu - cha - ris - tic feast.
Has re - deemed us by His blood."

Now, My Tongue, the Mystery Telling

852

1 Now, my tongue, the mys - t'ry tell - ing
2 Giv'n for us, and con - de - scend - ing
3 That last night at sup - per ly - ing
4 Word made flesh, the bread He tak - eth,

Of the glo - rious Bod - y sing,
To be born for us be - low,
Mid the Twelve, His cho - sen band,
By His word His Flesh to be;

And the Blood, all price ex - cell - ing,
He with us in con - verse blend - ing
Je - sus, with the Law com - ply - ing,
Wine His sa - cred Blood He mak - eth,

Which the Gen - tiles' Lord and King,
Dwelt, the seed of truth to sow,
Keeps the feast its rites de - mand;
Though the sens - es fail to see;

The shadows of the Passover find their reality and fulfillment in Christ, the true
Paschal Lamb, whose body and blood were given and shed on the cross to take
away the sin of the world. This hymn may be sung to FORTUNATUS NEW.

Text: Thomas Aquinas, 1225–74; tr. *Hymnal 1940*
Music: Plainsong Mode III; setting: Joseph Herl, b. 1959

Text: © Church Pension Fund, admin. Church Publishing, Inc.
Tune: Public domain   Setting: © 1998 Concordia Publishing House

PANGE LINGUA
87 87 87

1 Cor. 11:23–26; Matt. 26:26–28; John 1:1–3, 14

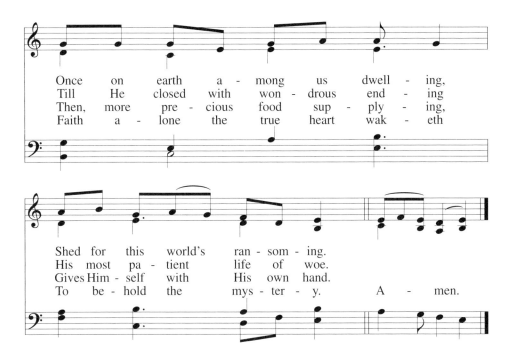

Once on earth a - mong us dwell - ing,
Till He closed with won - drous end - ing
Then, more pre - cious food sup - ply - ing,
Faith a - lone the true heart wak - eth

Shed for this world's ran - som - ing.
His most pa - tient life of woe.
Gives Him - self with His own hand.
To be - hold the mys - ter - y. A - men.

5 Glory let us give and blessing
   To the Father and the Son,
 Honor, thanks, and praise addressing,
   While eternal ages run;
 Ever too His love confessing
   Who from both with both is One.

853   The Infant Priest Was Holy Borne

1 The infant Priest was holy borne
  For us unholy and forlorn;
  From fleshly temple out came He,
  Anointed from eternity.

2 This great High Priest in human flesh
  Was icon of God's righteousness.
  His hallowed touch brought sanctity;
  His hand removed impurity.

3 The holy Lamb undaunted came
  To God's own altar lit with flame;
  While weeping angels hid their eyes,
  This Priest became a sacrifice.

4 But death would not the victor be
  Of Him who hung upon the tree.
  He leads us to the Holy Place
  Within the veil before God's face.

5 God's unveiled presence now we see,
  As at the rail on bended knee
  Our hungry mouths from Him receive
  The bread of immortality.

6 The body of God's Lamb we eat
  A priestly food and priestly meat.
  On sin-parched lips the chalice pours
  His quenching blood that life restores.

The Son of God was issued from the temple of Mary's womb as the great High Priest. His death as the true Lamb of God brings us life. We receive forgiveness of sins as we feed upon Christ's true body and blood in the Sacrament.

Text: Chad L. Bird, b. 1970
Music: Edward Miller, 1731–1807, adapt.

Text: © 1997 Chad L. Bird
Music: Public domain

ROCKINGHAM OLD
LM

Heb. 9:11–28; John 1:29; 6:51–58

Eat This Bread

854

Refrain

Eat this bread, drink this cup, come to Me and nev-er be hun-gry.

Eat this bread, drink this cup, trust in Me and you will not thirst.

Cantor or choir   *Refrain*

1 This is My bod-y giv-en for you; this is My blood that was shed for you.

2 As of-ten as you eat this bread and drink this cup, you show My death un-til I come a-gain.

3 Eat My flesh and drink My blood, and I will raise you up on the last day.

4 An-y one who eats this bread, will live for-ev-er.

5 If you be-lieve and eat this bread, you will have e-ter-nal life.

* Choose either part

Text: Robert Batastini, b. 1942, and the Taizé Community; sts. 1–2: Stephen P. Starke, b. 1955
Music: Jacques Berthier, 1923–94

Text (refrain and sts. 3–5) and music: Copyright © 1984 Les Presses de Taizé, admin. GIA Publications, Inc.
Text (sts. 1–2): © 1998 Concordia Publishing House

EAT THIS BREAD
Irregular

1 Cor. 11:23–26; John 6

855
You Satisfy the Hungry Heart

You sat-is-fy the hun-gry heart with gift of fin-est wheat.

Come give to us, O sav-ing Lord, the bread of life to eat.

1 As when the shep-herd calls his sheep, They know and heed his voice;
2 With joy-ful lips we sing to You Our praise and grat - i - tude
3 Is not the cup we bless and share The blood of Christ out- poured?
4 The mys-t'ry of Your pres-ence, Lord, No mor - tal tongue can tell:
5 You give Your-self to us, O Lord; Then self - less let us be,

So when You call Your fam-'ly, Lord, We fol - low and re - joice.
That You should count us wor-thy, Lord, To share this heav'n-ly food.
Do not one cup, one loaf, de - clare Our one - ness in the Lord?
Whom all the world can- not con - tain Comes in our hearts to dwell.
To serve each oth - er in Your name In truth and char - i - ty.

*All spiritual hunger is fully satisfied in the blessed meal Christ spreads
for the forgiveness of our sins. This text and tune help us to sing God's
praise for counting us worthy "to share this heav'nly food."*

Text: Omer Westendorf, 1916–97
Music: Robert Kreutz, 1922–96

BICENTENNIAL (FINEST WHEAT)
CM and refrain

 Ps. 81:16; 1 Cor. 10:16–17; John 10:2–4; 1 John 4:7–21

Come, Risen Lord

856

1 Come, ris - en Lord, and deign to be our guest;
2 We meet, as in that Up - per Room they met.
3 One bod - y we, one bod - y who par - take,
4 One with each oth - er, Lord, for one in Thee,

Nay, let us be Thy guests; the feast is Thine.
Thou at the ta - ble, bless - ing, yet dost stand.
One Church u - nit - ed in com - mu - nion blest,
Who art one Sav - ior and one liv - ing head.

Thy - self at Thine own board make man - i - fest
"This is My bod - y"; so Thou giv - est yet;
One name we bear, one bread of life we break,
Then o - pen Thou our eyes, that we may see;

In Thine own sac - ra - ment of bread and wine.
Faith still re - ceives the cup as from Thy hand.
With all Thy saints on earth and saints at rest.
Be known to us in break - ing of the bread.

As Jesus was made known to the Emmaus disciples in the breaking of the
bread, so He made known to us in the Supper of His body and blood.

Text: George W. Briggs, 1875–1959, alt.
Tune: Alfred M. Smith, 1879–1971; setting: Richard W. Hillert, b. 1923

Text: © Oxford University Press
Tune: © 1990 Church of the Ascension, Atlantic City, N.J.   Setting: © 1969 Concordia Publishing House

SURSUM CORDA
10 10 10 10

Mark 14:12–25; 1 Cor. 10:16–17; Luke 24:28–35

857 Jesus, Thy Boundless Love to Me

1 Je - sus, Thy bound-less love to me No thought can reach, no
2 Oh, grant that noth - ing in my soul May dwell, but Thy pure
3 This love un - wea - ried I pur-sue And daunt-less - ly to
4 In suf-f'ring be Thy love my peace, In weak-ness be Thy

tongue de - clare; U - nite my thank - ful heart to Thee,
love a - lone; Oh, may Thy love pos - sess me whole,
Thee as - pire. Oh, may Thy love my hope re - new,
love my pow'r; And when the storms of life shall cease,

And reign with-out a ri - val there! Thine whol-ly, Thine a -
My joy, my trea - sure, and my crown! All cold-ness from my
Burn in my soul like heav'n-ly fire! And day and night, be
O Je - sus, in that fi - nal hour, Be Thou my rod and

lone, I am; Be Thou a - lone my con - stant flame.
heart re - move; My ev - 'ry act, word, thought, be love.
all my care To guard this sa - cred trea - sure there.
staff and guide And draw me safe - ly to Thy side!

Text: Paul Gerhardt, 1607–76; tr. John Wesley, 1703–91, alt.
Music: Norman Cocker, 1889–1953

RYBURN
88 88 88

John 15:9–13; 1 John 4:7–19

O Jesus So Sweet, O Jesus So Mild   858

1 O Jesus so sweet, O Jesus so mild! For
2 O Jesus so sweet, O Jesus so mild! With
3 O Jesus so sweet, O Jesus so mild! Joy

sin-ners You be-came a child. You came from
God we now are rec-on-ciled. You have for
fills the world which sin de-filed. What-e'er we

heav-en to ful-fill Your Fa-ther's just and
all the ran-som paid, Your Fa-ther's righ-teous
have be-longs to You; Oh, keep us faith-ful,

ho-ly will. O Je-sus so sweet, O Je-sus so mild!
an-ger stayed. O Je-sus so sweet, O Je-sus so mild!
strong, and true. O Je-sus so sweet, O Je-sus so mild!

Text: Valentin Thilo, 1607–62, alt.; tr. Frieda Pietsch, alt.
Tune: *Ausserlesene, Catholische, Geistliche Kirchengesäng,* Köln, 1623, alt.; setting: J. S. Bach, 1685–1750

Text and music: Public domain

O JESULEIN SÜSS
10 8 88 10

Gal. 4:4–5; Rom. 5:8–11

859

When I Behold Jesus Christ

1 When I be-hold Je - sus Christ, True God who died for me,
2 For me You gave all Your love, For me You suf - fered pain;
3 You had no sin, ho - ly Lord, But You were tor - tured, tried;
4 What love is this? Great - er love No one has ev - er known.

I won-der much at His love As He hung on the tree.
I find no words, noth - ing can Your self - less-ness ex - plain.
On Gol - go - tha there for all My sins You bled and died.
My life with God— this I owe To You, and You a - lone.

Refrain

What kind of love is this? What kind of love is this?

You showed Your love, Je - sus, there To me on Cal - va - ry.

This hymn from Ethiopia explores the vicarious atonement: the sacrificial death of Jesus Christ on the cross in our place. Indeed, "what kind of love is this" that God took our sin upon Himself and died for us?!

Text: Almaz Belhu, sts. 1–3, tr. Hartmut Schoenherr with Jim and Aurelia Keefer, alt.; Joseph Herl, b. 1959, st. 4
Tune: Almaz Belhu; setting: Henry V. Gerike, b. 1948

MIN AYNET FAQIR NEW
76 76 and refrain

Text (sts. 1–3) and tune: © 1970 Ethiopian Evangelical Church MeKane Yesus; text (st. 4): © 1998 Concordia Publishing House
Setting: © 1998 Concordia Publishing House

1 John 4:9–10; John 15:13

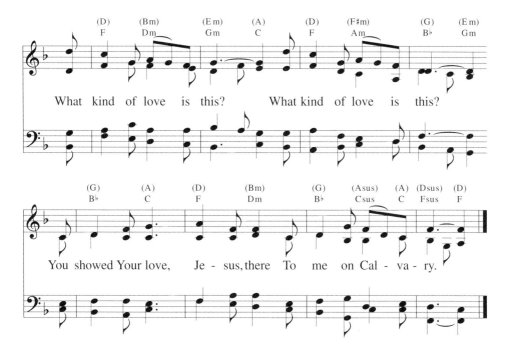

What kind of love is this? What kind of love is this?

You showed Your love, Je - sus, there To me on Cal - va - ry.

860   What Wondrous Love Is This

1 What won-drous love is this, O my soul, O my soul! What
2 When I was sink-ing down, sink-ing down, sink-ing down, When
3 To God and to the Lamb I will sing, I will sing; To
4 And when from death I'm free, I'll sing on, I'll sing on; And

won-drous love is this, O my soul! What won-drous love is this That
I was sink-ing down, sink-ing down, When I was sink-ing down Be-
God and to the Lamb I will sing; To God and to the Lamb, Who
when from death I'm free, I'll sing on. And when from death I'm free I'll

caused the Lord of bliss To bear the dread-ful curse for my
neath God's right-eous frown, Christ laid a-side His crown for my
is the great I AM, While mil-lions join the theme, I will
sing His love for me, And through e-ter-ni-ty I'll sing

soul, for my soul, To bear the dread-ful curse for my soul!
soul, for my soul, Christ laid a-side His crown for my soul.
sing, I will sing, While mil-lions join the theme, I will sing.
on, I'll sing on, And through e-ter-ni-ty I'll sing on.

*This haunting early-American tune supports this meditative text on the love
of God for us in Christ. The wondrous love of God caused the incarnation
of our Lord, culminating in Jesus' substitutionary death for us.*

Text: American folk hymn, *A General Selection of … Spiritual Songs,* Lynchburg, 1811, alt.
Tune: *Southern Harmony,* New Haven, 1835; setting: Donald A. Busarow, b. 1934

WONDROUS LOVE
12 9 66 12 9

1 John 4:7–10; Rev. 5:6–13; John 8:58

No Temple Now, No Gift of Price 861

1 No tem-ple now, no gift of price, No priest-ly round of
2 The dy-ing Lord our ran-som paid, One fi-nal full self-
3 In faith and con-fi-dence draw near, With-in the ho-li-
4 For Christ is ours! With pur-pose true The pil-grim path of

sac-ri-fice, Re-tain their an-cient pow'rs. As
off-'ring made, Com-plete in ev-'ry part. His
est ap-pear, With all who praise and pray; Who
faith pur-sue, The road that Je-sus trod; Un-

shad-ows fade be-fore the sun The day of sac-ri-
fin-ished sac-ri-fice for sins The cov-e-nant of
share one fam-i-ly, one feast, One great im-per-ish-
til by His pre-vail-ing grace We stand at last be-

fice is done, The day of grace is ours.
grace be-gins, The law with-in the heart.
a-ble Priest, One new and liv-ing way.
fore His face, Our Sav-ior and our God.

Christ was the reality foreshadowed by the Old Testament priesthood, sacrificial system, and temple. This new tune by Joseph Herl underscores Timothy Dudley-Smith's text based on the rich imagery from the book of Hebrews.

Text: Timothy Dudley-Smith, b. 1926
Music: Joseph Herl, b. 1959

KIRKWOOD
886 886

Heb. 9:11–28; 10:10–22; Jer. 31:31–34

All Praise to Thee,
for Thou, O King Divine

1 All praise to Thee, for Thou, O King di - vine,
2 Thou cam'st to us in low - li - ness of thought;
3 Let this mind be in us which was in Thee,
4 Where-fore, by God's e - ter - nal pur - pose, Thou
5 Let ev - 'ry tongue con - fess with one ac - cord,

Didst yield the glo - ry that of right was Thine,
By Thee the out - cast and the poor were sought;
Who wast a ser - vant that we might be free,
Art high ex - al - ted o'er all crea - tures now,
In heav'n and earth, that Je - sus Christ is Lord,

That in our dark - ened hearts Thy grace might shine.
And by Thy death was God's sal - va - tion wrought.
Hum-bling Thy - self to death on Cal - va - ry.
And giv'n the name to which all knees shall bow.
And God the Fa - ther be by all a - dored.

Al - le - lu - ia! Al - le - lu - ia!

Text: F. Bland Tucker, 1895–1984
Music: Charles V. Stanford, 1852–1924

Text: © Church Pension Fund, admin. Church Publishing, Inc.
Music: Public domain

ENGELBERG
10 10 10 4

Phil. 2:5–11; Mark 10:45; Is. 55:10–11

This Is the Threefold Truth

863

1 This is the three-fold truth on which our faith de - pends;
2 Made sa - cred by long use, new - mint - ed for our time,
3 On this we fix our minds as, kneel - ing side by side,
4 By this we are up - held when doubt or grief as - sails
5 This is the three-fold truth which, if we hold it fast,

And with this joy - ful cry___ wor - ship be-gins and ends:
Our lit - ur - gies sum up the hope we___ have in Him:
We take the bread and wine—take Him, the___ Cru - ci - fied:
Our Chris - tian faith and love, and on - ly___ grace a - vails:
Chang - es the world and us and brings us___ home at last:

Refrain

Christ has died! Christ is ris - en! Christ will come a - gain!

Text: Fred Pratt Green, b. 1903, alt.
Music: Jack Schrader, b. 1942

Text and music: © 1980 Hope Publishing Co.

ACCLAMATIONS
12 12 12

1 Cor. 11:23–26

864 Church of God, Elect and Glorious

1 Church of God, e - lect and glo - rious, Ho - ly
2 God has called you out of dark - ness In - to
3 Once you were an al - ien peo - ple, Stran - gers
4 Church of God, e - lect and ho - ly, Be the

na - tion, cho - sen race; Called as God's own
His most mar - v'lous light; Brought His truth to
to God's heart of love; But He brought you
peo - ple He in - tends; Strong in faith and

spe - cial peo - ple, Roy - al priests and heirs of
life with - in you, Turned your blind - ness in - to
home in mer - cy, Cit - i - zens of heav'n a -
swift to an - swer Each com - mand your mas - ter

grace: Know the pur - pose of your call - ing,
sight. Let your light so shine a - round you
bove. Let His love flow out to oth - ers,
sends: Roy - al priests, ful - fill your call - ing

Drawing on rich New Testament imagery that describes the Church,
this hymn recalls our priestly status as the chosen people of God.

Text: James E. Seddon, 1915–83
Music: Cyril V. Taylor, 1907–92

Text: © 1982 Hope Publishing Co.
Music: © 1942, renewal 1970 Hope Publishing Co.

ABBOT'S LEIGH
87 87 D

1 Peter 2:9–10; Eph. 2:19–22; Rev. 5:9–10

Show to all His might - y deeds; Tell of love that
That God's name is glo - ri - fied; And all find fresh
Let them feel a Fa - ther's care; That they too may
Through your sac - ri - fice and prayer; Give your lives in

knows no lim - its, Grace that meets all hu - man needs.
hope and pur-pose In Christ Je - sus cru - ci - fied.
know His wel-come And His count - less bless - ings share.
joy - ful ser-vice— Sing His praise, His love de - clare.

865 Christ Is Made the Sure Foundation

1 Christ is made the sure foun-da-tion, Christ, our head and
2 To this tem-ple, where we call You, Come, O Lord of
3 Grant, we pray, to all Your faith-ful All the gifts they
4 Praise and hon-or to the Fa-ther, Praise and hon - or

cor - ner - stone, Cho - sen of the Lord and pre - cious,
hosts, and stay; Come with all Your lov - ing-kind - ness,
ask to gain; What they gain from You, for - ev - er
to the Son, Praise and hon - or to the Spir - it,

Bind - ing all the Church in one; Ho - ly Zi - on's
Hear Your peo - ple as they pray; And Your full - est
With the bless - ed to re - tain; And here - af - ter
Ev - er three and ev - er one: One in might and

help for-ev - er And our con - fi - dence a - lone.
ben - e - dic - tion Shed with-in these walls to - day.
in Your glo - ry Ev - er-more with You to reign.
one in glo - ry While un-end - ing a - ges run!

Gathered around Word and Sacrament, our lives are securely grounded on the one true foundation of the Church. This sturdy tune depicts the strength of Christ as He supports His Church.

Text: Latin hymn, c. 7th cent.; tr. John M. Neale, 1818–1866, alt.
Music: Henry Purcell, 1659–95, alt.

WESTMINSTER ABBEY
87 87 87

Text and music: Public domain

1 Peter 2:5–7; Revelation 21; Eph. 2:20–22; Is. 28:16

Be Strong in the Lord

866

1 Be strong in the Lord in ar - mor of light!
2 In - teg - ri - ty gird you round to im - part
3 With ea - ger - ness shod stand firm in your place,
4 Though Sa - tan pre - sume to test you and try,
5 So wield well your blade, re - joice in its pow'rs!

With hel - met and sword, with shield for the fight;
The truth of His Word as truth in your heart:
Or go forth for God with news of His grace:
In hel - met and plume your head shall be high:
Fight on un - dis - mayed for Je - sus is ours!

On prayer be de - pen - dent, be belt - ed and shod,
His righ - teous - ness wear - ing as breast - plate of mail,
No foe shall dis - arm you nor force you to yield,
Be - set by temp - ta - tion be true to your Lord,
Then in Him vic - to - rious your ar - mor lay down,

In breast - plate re - splen - dent— the ar - mor of God.
His vic - to - ry shar - ing, be strong to pre - vail.
No ar - row can harm you with faith as your shield.
Your hel - met sal - va - tion and Scrip - ture your sword.
To praise, ev - er glo - rious, His cross and His crown.

God gives Christians spiritual armor to aid them in their struggle against sin,
death, and the devil. This text, a sermon in poetry based on Ephesians 6, reminds us
that we gain the victory over all our spiritual enemies in and through Jesus Christ.

Text: Timothy Dudley-Smith, b. 1926
Music: C. Hubert H. Parry, 1848–1918

Text: © 1984 by Hope Publishing Co.
Music: Public domain

LAUDATE DOMINUM
10 10 11 11

Eph. 6:10–18; 1 Peter 5:8–10

867   Thine the Amen, Thine the Praise

1 Thine the a - men Thine the praise Al - le -
2 Thine the life e - ter - nal - ly Thine the
3 Thine the tru - ly Thine the yes Thine the
4 Thine the king - dom Thine the prize Thine the
5 Thine the glo - ry in the night No more

lu - ias an - gels raise Thine the ev - er - last - ing head
prom-ise let there be Thine the vi - sion Thine the tree
ta - ble we the guest Thine the mer - cy all from Thee
won - der full sur - prise Thine the ban - quet then the praise
dy - ing on - ly light Thine the riv - er Thine the tree

Thine the break - ing of the bread Thine the glo - ry Thine the
All the earth on bend - ed knee Gone the nail - ing gone the
Thine the glo - ry yet to be Then the ring - ing and the
Then the jus - tice of Thy ways Thine the glo - ry Thine the
Then the Lamb e - ter - nal - ly Then the ho - ly ho - ly

Text: Herbert F. Brokering, b. 1926
Music: Carl F. Schalk, b. 1929

THINE
77 77 87 14

    Matt. 26:26–29; Rev. 19:9–16

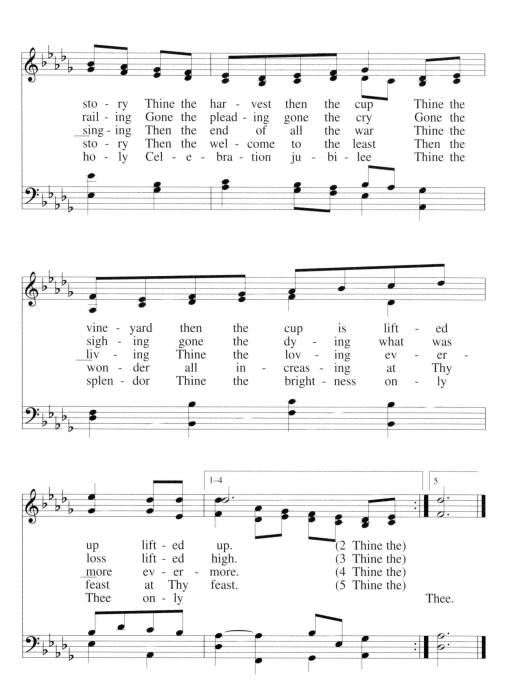

sto - ry Thine the har - vest then the cup Thine the
rail - ing Gone the plead - ing gone the cry Gone the
sing - ing Then the end of all the war Thine the
sto - ry Then the wel - come to the least Then the
ho - ly Cel - e - bra - tion ju - bi - lee Thine the

vine - yard then the cup is lift - ed
sigh - ing gone the dy - ing what was
liv - ing Thine the lov - ing ev - er -
won - der all in - creas - ing at Thy
splen - dor Thine the bright - ness on - ly

up lift - ed up. (2 Thine the)
loss lift - ed high. (3 Thine the)
more ev - er - more. (4 Thine the)
feast at Thy feast. (5 Thine the)
Thee on - ly Thee.

868

"How Shall They Hear," Who Have Not Heard

1 "How shall they hear," who have not heard
2 "To all the world," to ev - 'ry place,
3 "Whom shall I send?" Who hears the call,
4 "Lord, here am I": Your fire im - part
5 Spir - it of love, with - in us move:

News of a Lord who loved and came;
Neigh-bors and friends and far - off lands,
Con - stant in prayer, through toil and pain,
To this poor cold self - cen - tered soul;
Spir - it of truth, in pow'r come down!

Nor known His rec - on - cil - ing word,
Preach the good news of sav - ing grace;
Tell - ing of One who died for all,
Touch but my lips, my hands, my heart,
So shall they hear and find and prove

Nor learned to trust a Sav - ior's name?
Go while the great com - mis - sion stands.
To bring a lost world home a - gain?
And make a world for Christ my goal.
Christ is their life, their joy, their crown.

*The apostle Paul's mission impetus and the call and response of the prophet
Isaiah are here joined together by the hymnwriter, encouraging Christians
to take seriously their vocation of making disciples of every nation.*

Text: Timothy Dudley-Smith, b. 1926
Music: *Cantica Spiritualia*, 1847

ANGELUS (DU MEINER SEELEN)
LM

Rom. 10:14–15; Matt. 28:18–20; Is. 6:5–8; Acts 4:29–31

O God of Light

869

1 O God of light, Your Word, a lamp un-fail-ing,
2 From days of old, through blind and will-ful a-ges,
3 Un-dimmed by time, those words are still re-veal-ing,
4 To all the world Your sum-mons You are send-ing,

Shall pierce the dark-ness of our earth-bound way
Though we re-belled, You gent-ly sought a-gain,
To sin-ful hearts Your jus-tice and Your grace;
Through all the earth, to ev-'ry land and race,

And show Your grace, Your plan for us un-veil-ing,
And spoke through saints, a-pos-tles, proph-ets, sa-ges,
And quest-ing spir-its, long-ing for Your heal-ing,
That myr-iad tongues, in one great an-them blend-ing,

And guide our foot-steps to the per-fect day.
Who wrote with ea-ger or re-luc-tant pen.
See Your com-pas-sion in the Sav-ior's face.
May praise and cel-e-brate Your gift of grace.

Text: Sarah Taylor, 1883–1954, alt.
Music: H. Barrie Cabena, b. 1933

Text: © 1952, renewal 1980 The Hymn Society, admin. Hope Publishing Co.
Music: © 1978 *Lutheran Book of Worship*

ATKINSON
11 10 11 10

Ps. 119:105; 1 Peter 1:10–12; Is. 51:4

870 Surely It Is God Who Saves Me

A paraphrase of "The First Song of Isaiah," an Old Testament hymn of praise, this hymn encourages us to go and tell all people the great things God has done.

Text: Carl P. Daw, Jr., b. 1944
Music: Ray W. Urwin, b. 1950

Text: © 1982 Hope Publishing Co.
Music: © 1984 Ray W. Urwin

THOMAS MERTON
87 87 D

Is. 12:2–6

871

Rise, Shine, You People

1 Rise, shine, you peo - ple! Christ the Lord has en - tered
2 See how He sends the pow'rs of e - vil reel - ing;
3 Come, cel - e - brate, your ban - ners high un - furl - ing,
4 Tell how the Fa - ther sent His Son to save us.

Our hu - man sto - ry; God in Him is cen - tered.
He brings us free - dom, light and life and heal - ing.
Your songs and prayers a - gainst the dark - ness hurl - ing.
Tell of the Son, who life and free - dom gave us.

He comes to us, by death and sin sur -
All men and wom - en, who by guilt are
To all the world go out and tell the
Tell how the Spir - it calls from ev - 'ry

round - ed, With grace un - bound - ed.
driv - en, Now are for - giv - en.
sto - ry Of Je - sus' glo - ry.
na - tion His new cre - a - tion.

Text: Ronald A. Klug, b. 1939
Music: Dale Wood, b. 1934

WOJTKIEWIECZ
11 11 11 5

Eph. 5:14; Col. 2:13–15

Listen, God Is Calling

872

The leader's call to "listen" summons us to pay attention to God's call through His Word. Just as the one-beat measures interupt the rhythm, so does God's call break into our lives and demand that we "listen."

Text: Kenyan traditional; tr. Howard S. Olson, b. 1922
Tune: Kenyan traditional; setting: Austin C. Lovelace, b. 1919

NENO LAKE MUNGU
64 64 and refrain

Mark 16:15; Matt. 28:18–20

873

The Tree of Life

1 The tree of life with ev-'ry good In E-den's
2 The still-ness of that sa-cred grove Was bro-ken,
3 What mer-cy God showed to our race, A plan of
4 Now from that tree of Je-sus' shame Flows life e-

ho-ly or-chard stood, And of its fruit so pure and
as the ser-pent strove With tempt-ing voice to Eve be-
res-cue by His grace: In send-ing One from wom-an's
ter-nal in His name; For all who trust and will be-

sweet God let the man and wom-an eat. Yet in this
guile And Ad-am too by sin de-file. O day of
seed, The One to fill our great-est need— For on a
lieve, Sal-va-tion's liv-ing fruit re-ceive. And of this

gar-den al-so grew An-oth-er tree, of which they
sad-ness when the breath Of fear and dark-ness, doubt and
tree up-lift-ed high His on-ly Son for sin would
fruit so pure and sweet The Lord in-vites the world to

*The cross of Christ is the tree of life, in which are found all the blessings
of eternal life and salvation. God now invites all people to freely eat of
its pure and living fruit so that they too might enjoy such blessings.*

Text: Stephen P. Starke, b. 1955
Music: Bruce W. Becker, b. 1952

Text: © 1993 Stephen P. Starke
Music: © 1995 Bruce W. Becker

TREE OF LIFE
88 88 88 88

Gen. 3:1–15; Rev. 22:1–3; 1 Peter 2:24

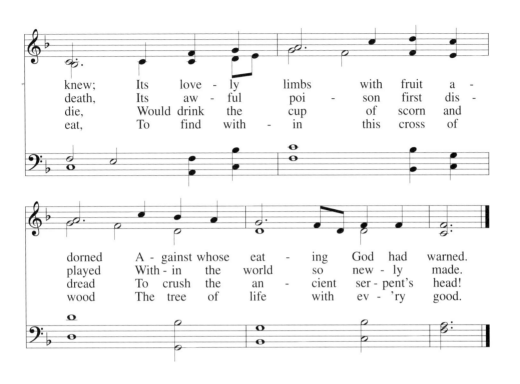

knew; Its love - ly limbs with fruit a -
death, Its aw - ful poi - son first dis -
die, Would drink the cup of scorn and
eat, To find with - in this cross of

dorned A - gainst whose eat - ing God had warned.
played With - in the world so new - ly made.
dread To crush the an - cient ser - pent's head!
wood The tree of life with ev - 'ry good.

874

Not unto Us

1 Not un - to us, not un - to us be glo - ry,
2 A - maz - ing grace— that chose us e'er the worlds were
3 O faith - ful love— that shep - herd - ed through faith - less
4 Not un - to us but to Your name be glo - ry,

Lord; Not un - to us but to Your name be
made; A - maz - ing grace— that sent Your Son to
years; For - giv - ing love— that led us to Your
Lord, For grace so rich, so wide, so high, so

praise; Not un - to us but to Your name all hon - or be
save; A - maz - ing grace— that robed us in Your righ - teous -
truth; Un - yield - ing love— that would not let us turn from
free. A - bide with us till trav - 'ling days are o - ver and

giv'n For match - less mer - cy, for - give - ness, and grace.
ness And taught our lips to sing glo - ry and praise.
You But sent us forth to speak par - don and peace.
done, And pil - grim feet lead us home, Lord, to You.

*Both text and tune are contributed by Lutheran music scholar Kurt
Eggert. The hymn focuses on the unfathomable love and mercy of
God who, as our Redeemer, deserves all glory and praise.*

Text: Kurt J. Eggert, 1923–93
Music: Kurt J. Eggert, 1923–93

NOT UNTO US
12 10 13 10

Text and music: © 1993 Kurt J. Eggert, admin. Ruth Eggert

Ps. 115:1; Eph. 3:21; Phil. 3:8–9; Heb. 11:13–16

Fruitful Trees, the Spirit's Sowing 875

1 Fruit - ful trees, the Spir - it's sow - ing, May we rip - en
2 Lad - en branch - es free - ly bear - ing Gifts the Giv - er
3 Root - ed deep in Christ our Mas - ter, Christ our pat - tern
4 Fruit - ful trees, the Spir - it's tend - ing, May we grow till

and in - crease, Fruit to life e - ter - nal grow - ing,
loves to bless; Here is fruit that grows by shar - ing:
and our goal, Teach us, as the years fly fast - er,
har - vests cease; Till we taste, in life un - end - ing,

Rich in love and joy and peace.
Pa - tience, kind - ness, gen - tle - ness.
Good - ness, faith and self - con - trol.
Heav - en's love and joy and peace.

The texts of British hymnwriter Timothy Dudley-Smith cover a broad range of
biblical accounts and topics. Here the ninefold fruit of the Spirit provides the
impetus for prayer to God that such heavenly graces would adorn our lives.

Text: Timothy Dudley-Smith, b. 1929
Music: Ralph C. Schultz, b. 1932

Text: © 1984 Hope Publishing Co.
Tune: © 1980 Concordia Publishing House   Setting: © 1998 Concordia Publishing House

DOROTHY
87 87

Gal. 5:22–23; John 15:1–9

876 Come, Thou Fount of Every Blessing

1 Come, Thou Fount of ev - 'ry bless - ing, Tune my heart to sing Thy grace;
2 Here I raise my Eb - en - e - zer, Hith - er by Thy help I've come;
3 Oh, to grace how great a debt - or Dai - ly I'm con - strained to be;
4 Oh, that day when freed from sin - ning, I shall see Thy love - ly face;

Streams of mer - cy, nev - er ceas - ing, Call for songs of loud - est praise.
And I hope, by Thy good plea - sure, Safe - ly to ar - rive at home.
Let that grace now like a fet - ter Bind my wan - d'ring heart to Thee:
Clothed then in the blood-washed lin - en How I'll sing Thy won-drous grace!

While the hope of end - less glo - ry Fills my heart with joy and love,
Je - sus sought me when a strang - er, Wan - d'ring from the fold of God;
Prone to wan - der, Lord, I feel it; Prone to leave the God I love.
Come, my Lord, no long - er tar - ry, Take my ran - som'd soul a - way;

Teach me ev - er to a - dore Thee; May I still Thy good - ness prove.
He, to res - cue me from dan - ger, In - ter - posed His pre - cious blood.
Here's my heart, oh, take and seal it, Seal it for Thy courts a - bove.
Send Thine an - gels soon to car - ry Me to realms of end - less day.

*Ebenezer means "Thus far has the Lord helped us" and was the name given to the
stone of remembrance that Samuel raised to God's glory. God has gained the victory for
us, and we now look to a far greater monument recalling our deliverance: the cross.*

Text: Robert Robinson, 1735–90, alt.
Music: John Wyeth's *Repository of Sacred Music*, 1813

NETTLETON
87 87 D

John 7:37–39; Is. 55:1–2; 1 Sam. 7:3–12

"Forgive Our Sins as We Forgive" 877

1 "For - give our sins as we for - give," You
2 How can Your par - don reach and bless The
3 In blaz - ing light Your cross re - veals The
4 Lord, cleanse the depths with - in our souls And

taught us, Lord, to pray, But You a - lone can
un - for - giv - ing heart That broods on wrongs and
truth we dim - ly knew: What triv - ial debts are
bid re - sent - ment cease. Then, bound to all in

grant us grace To live the words we say.
will not let Old bit - ter - ness de - part?
owed to us, How great our debt to You.
bonds of love, Our lives will spread Your peace.

Text: Rosamond E. Herklots, 1905–87, alt.
Music: *A Supplement to the Kentucky Harmony,* 1820; setting: Kenneth T. Kosche, b. 1947

DETROIT
CM

Matt. 6:12; 18:21–35; Eph. 4:31–32

878   Where Charity and Love Prevail

1 Where char - i - ty and love pre - vail There
2 With grate - ful joy and ho - ly fear His
3 For - give we now each oth - er's faults As
4 Let strife a - mong us be un - known; Let

God is ev - er found; Brought here to - geth - er
char - i - ty we learn; Let us with heart and
we our faults con - fess, And let us love each
all con - ten - tion cease; Be God's the glo - ry

by Christ's love By love are we thus bound.
mind and soul Now love Him in re - turn.
oth - er well In Chris - tian ho - li - ness.
that we seek; Be ours His ho - ly peace.

5 Let us recall that in our midst
  Dwells Christ, His only Son;
As members of His Body joined
  We are in Him made one.

6 For love excludes no race or clan
  That names the Savior's Name;
His family embraces all
  Whose Father is the same.

Text: Latin hymn, 9th century; tr. Omer Westendorf, 1916–97, alt.
Music: Lucius Chapin, 1760–1842

Text: © 1960 World Library Publications
Music: Public domain

TWENTY-FOURTH (PRIMROSE)
CM

John 13:1–17; 1 John 4:7–21; Eph. 4:29–32

How Clear Is Our Vocation, Lord 879

1 How clear is our vo - ca - tion, Lord, When
2 But if, for - get - ful, we should find Your
3 We mar - vel how Your saints be - come In
4 In what You give us, Lord, to do, To -

once we heed Your call: To live ac - cord - ing
yoke is hard to bear; If world - ly pres - sures
hin - dranc - es more sure; Whose joy - ful vir - tues
geth - er or a - lone, In old rou - tines or

to Your Word, And dai - ly learn, re - freshed, re - stored, That
fray the mind, And love it - self can - not un - wind Its
put to shame The cas - ual way we wear Your name, And
ven - tures new, May we not cease to look to You, The

You are Lord of all, And will not let us fall.
tan - gled skein of care: Our in - ward life re - pair.
by our faults ob - scure Your pow'r to cleanse and cure.
cross You hung up - on— All You en - deav - ored done.

*With a variety of wonderful poetic images, Fred Pratt Green reminds Christians of
their calling in life as it is lived under the cross. The "skein" (pronounced SKANE)
in stanza 2 reminds us that we depend on God to untangle our sin-filled lives.*

Text: Fred Pratt Green, b. 1903
Music: C. Hubert H. Parry, 1848–1918, alt.

REPTON
86 88 66

Luke 5:1–11; Matt. 11:28–30; Heb. 12:1–4

880   For All the Faithful Women

1 For all the faith-ful wom'-en Who served in days of old,
2 *Insert appropriate stanza(s).*
3 O God, for saints and ser-vants, Those named and those un-known
4 All praise to God the Fa-ther! All praise to Christ the Son!

To You shall thanks be giv-en; To all, their sto-ry told.

In whom, through all the a-ges, Your light of glo-ry shone,
All praise, the Ho-ly Spir-it, Who binds the Church as one!

They served with strength and glad-ness In tasks Your wis-dom gave.

We of-fer glad thanks-giv-ing And fer-vent prayer we raise
With saints who went be-fore us, With saints who wit-ness still,

To You their lives bore wit-ness, Pro-claimed Your pow'r to save.

That, faith-ful in Your ser-vice, Our lives may sing Your praise.
We sing glad al-le-lu-ias And strive to do Your will.

This hymn highlights some of the Old and New Testament women of faith.
The appropriate stanza may be inserted as the second stanza of this hymn.
Many of these stanzas were written specifically for this supplement.

Text: Herman G. Stuempfle, Jr., b. 1923
Tune: Finnish folk; setting: Joseph Herl, b. 1959

KUORTANE (NYLAND)
76 76 D

Miriam

5 We praise Your name for Miriam
   Who sang triumphantly
While Pharoah's vaunted army
   Lay drowned beneath the sea.
As Israel marched to freedom,
   Her chains of bondage gone,
So may we reach the kingdom
   Your mighty arm has won.

Exodus 15:19–21

Deborah

6 All praise for that brave warrior
   Who fought at Your command.
You made her Israel's savior
   When foes oppressed the land.
As Deborah stood with valor
   Upon the battlefield,
May we, in evil's hour,
   Truth's sword with boldness wield.

Judges 4–5

Hannah

7 To Hannah, praying childless
   Before Your throne of grace,
You gave a son and called him
   To serve before Your face.
Grant us her perseverance;
   Lord, teach us how to pray
And trust in Your deliverance
   When darkness hides our way.

1 Samuel 1:1–2:10

Ruth

8 For Ruth who left her homeland
   And ventured forth in faith,
Who pledged to serve and worship
   Naomi's God 'til death,
We praise You, God of Israel
   And pray for hearts set free
To bind ourselves to others
   In love and loyalty.

Ruth 1:8–18

Mary, Mother of Our Lord

9 We sing of Mary, mother,
   Fair maiden, full of grace.
She bore the Christ, our brother,
   Who came to save our race.
May we, with her, surrender
   Ourselves to Your command
And lay upon Your altar
   Our gifts of heart and hand.

Luke 1:26–38

Martha and Mary

10 We sing of busy Martha
   Who toiled with pot and pan
While Mary sat in silence
   To hear the Word again.
Christ, keep our hearts attentive
   To truth that You declare,
And strengthen us for service
   When work becomes our prayer.

Luke 10:38–42

The Woman at the Well

11 Recall the outcast woman
   With whom the Lord conversed,
Christ gave her living water
   To quench her deepest thirst.
Like hers, our hearts are yearning;
   Christ offers us His Word.
Then may our lips be burning
   To witness to our Lord.

John 4:1–42

Mary Magdalene

12 We praise the other Mary
   Who came at Easter dawn
To look for Jesus' body
   And found her Lord was gone.
But, as with joy she saw Him
   In resurrection light,
May we by faith behold Him,
   The Day who ends our night!

John 20:10–18

Dorcas

13 Lord, hear our praise of Dorcas
   Who served the sick and poor.
Her hands were cups of kindness,
   Her heart an open door.
Send us, O Christ, Your Body,
   Where people cry in pain,
And touch them with compassion
   To make them whole again.

Acts 9:36

Praise the One
Who Breaks the Darkness

881

1 Praise the One who breaks the dark - ness With a lib - er - a - ting light; Praise the One who frees the pris - 'ners, Turn-ing blind-ness in - to sight. Praise the One who preached the Gos - pel, Heal - ing ev - 'ry dread dis - ease, Calm-ing

2 Praise the One who bless'd the chil - dren With a strong, yet gen - tle, word; Praise the One who drove out de - mons With the pierc-ing, two-edged sword. Praise the One who brings cool wa - ter To the des - ert's burn - ing sand; From this

3 Let us praise the Word in - car - nate, Christ, who suf - fered in our place; Je - sus died and rose vic - to - rious That we may know God by grace. Let us sing for joy and glad - ness, See - ing what our God has done; Let us

Text: Rusty Edwards, b. 1955
Music: *The Sacred Harp*, Philadelphia, 1844; setting: Ronald A. Nelson, b. 1927

Text: © 1987 Hope Publishing Co.
Tune: Public domain   Setting: © 1978 *Lutheran Book of Worship*

BEACH SPRING
87 87 D

Luke 4:16–21; Mark 10:13–16; John 1:1, 14, 29; 4:5–14

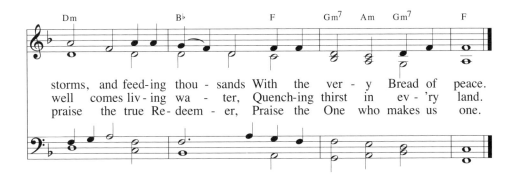

storms, and feed-ing thou - sands With the ver - y Bread of peace.
well comes liv - ing wa - ter, Quench-ing thirst in ev - 'ry land.
praise the true Re-deem - er, Praise the One who makes us one.

Lord, Whose Love through Humble Service — 882

1 Lord, whose love through humble service
    Bore the weight of human need,
Who upon the cross, forsaken,
    Offered mercy's perfect deed,
We, Your servants, bring the worship
    Not of voice alone, but heart,
Consecrating to Your purpose
    Ev'ry gift that You impart.

2 Still Your children wander homeless;
    Still the hungry cry for bread;
Still the captives long for freedom;
    Still in grief we mourn our dead.
As, O Lord, Your deep compassion
    Healed the sick and freed the soul,
Use the love Your Spirit kindles
    Still to save and make us whole.

3 As we worship, grant us vision,
    Till Your love's revealing light
In its height and depth and greatness,
    Dawns upon our quickened sight,
Making known the needs and burdens
    Your compassion bids us bear,
Stirring us to tireless striving,
    Your abundant life to share.

4 Called by worship to Your service,
    Forth in Your dear name we go,
To the child, the youth, the aged,
    Love in living deeds to show;
Hope and health, good will and comfort,
    Counsel, aid, and peace we give,
That Your servants, Lord, in freedom
    May Your mercy know and live.

The example of Christ's ministry to those in need is one believers can model as they become agents of healing and hope in society, living embodiments of the Gospel to people of all ages and in every condition. This hymn is to be sung to BEACH SPRING.

Text: Albert Bayly, 1901–84, alt.

Text: © Oxford University Press

Rom. 12:1; Matt. 25:34–40; Gal. 6:10

883 Weary of All Trumpeting

1 Wea - ry of all trum - pet - ing, Wea - ry of all kill - ing,
2 Cap - tain Christ, O low - ly Lord, Ser - vant King, Your dy - ing
3 To the tri - umph of Your cross Sum - mon all the liv - ing;

Wea - ry of all songs that sing Prom - ise, non - ful - fill - ing,
Bade us sheathe the fool - ish sword, Bade us cease de - ny - ing.
Sum - mon us to live by loss, Gain - ing all by giv - ing,

We would raise, O Christ, one song; We would join in sing - ing
Trum - pet with Your Spir - it's breath Through each height and hol - low;
Suf - f'ring all, that we may see Tri - umph in sur - ren - der;

That great mu - sic pure and strong, Where - with heav'n is ring - ing.
In - to Your self - giv - ing death, Call us all to fol - low.
Leav - ing all, that we may be Part - ners in Your splen - dor.

This melody by Hugo Distler was originally used as a military marching tune. Here
wonderfully redeemed by means of its juxtaposition with Martin Franzmann's text,
this hymn encourages us to follow Christ in a life of peace and self-sacrifice.

Text: Martin H. Franzmann, 1907–76, alt.
Tune: Hugo Distler, 1908–42; setting: Richard Proulx, b. 1937

Text and tune: © 1972 Chantry Music Press, admin. Augsburg Fortress
Setting: © 1975 GIA Publications, Inc.

DISTLER
76 76 D

Col. 2:8–10; Mark 8:34–38; 10:45; 1 Peter 4:12–16

Lord of All Good

884

1 Lord of all good, our gifts we bring You now;
2 We give our minds to un - der - stand Your ways;
3 Fa - ther, whose boun - ty all cre - a - tion shows;

Use them Your ho - ly pur - pose to ful - fill.
Hands, eyes, and voice to serve Your great de - sign;
Christ, by whose will - ing sac - ri - fice we live;

To - kens of love and pledg - es they shall be
Hearts with the flame of Your own love a - blaze—
Spir - it, from whom all life in full - ness flows:

That our whole life is of - fered to Your will.
Thus for Your glo - ry all our pow'rs com - bine.
To You with grate - ful hearts our - selves we give.

Text: Albert Bayly, 1901–84, alt.
Tune: Henry Lawes, 1595–1662; setting: Carl F. Schalk, b. 1929

Text: © Oxford University Press
Tune: Public domain   Setting: © 1969 Concordia Publishing House

FARLEY CASTLE
10 10 10 10

Rom. 12:1; 1 Peter 4:10–11

885 The Temple Rang with Golden Coins

1 The tem - ple rang with gold - en coins The rich in bright ar - ray Con - trib - ut - ed from gleam - ing hoards Their scales could scarce - ly weigh.

2 A wid - ow came with cop - per coins And of - fered them in praise. They were the last she had to give Or save for dark - er days.

3 When Je - sus saw her cost - ly gift And knew she had no more, He praised a love that spared not self And called her rich, though poor.

4 At last He brought His of - fer - ing And laid it on a tree; There gave Him - self, His life, His love For all hu - man - i - ty.

5 Lord, help us all, with You, to yield What - ev - er love de - mands And free - ly give, as You have giv'n, With o - pen hearts and hands.

True motivation for all biblical stewardship flows from the Gospel—Christ's sacrifice on the cross for all people—a point brought out by this text based on the account of the widow's mite.

Text: Herman G. Stuempfle, Jr., b. 1923
Tune: *Day's Psalter,* 1562; setting: Richard Redhead, 1820–1901

ST. FLAVIAN
CM

Text: Copyright © 1993 GIA Publications, Inc.
Music: Public domain

Mark 12:41–44; Heb. 10:4–12

Lord of All Hopefulness

886

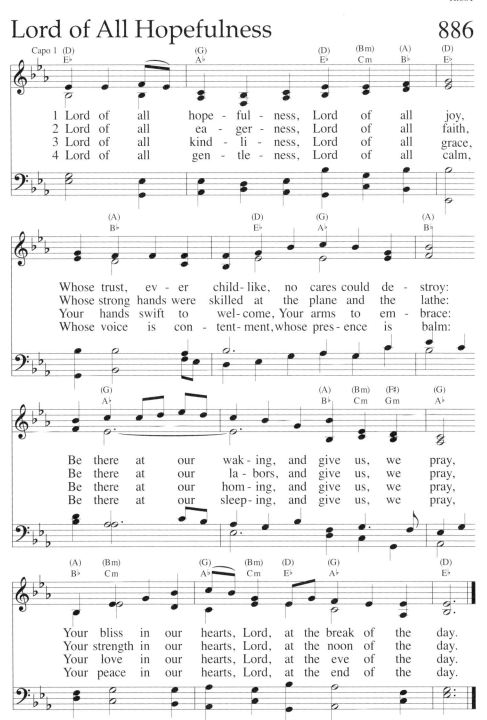

1 Lord of all hope - ful - ness, Lord of all joy,
2 Lord of all ea - ger - ness, Lord of all faith,
3 Lord of all kind - li - ness, Lord of all grace,
4 Lord of all gen - tle - ness, Lord of all calm,

Whose trust, ev - er child- like, no cares could de - stroy:
Whose strong hands were skilled at the plane and the lathe:
Your hands swift to wel - come, Your arms to em - brace:
Whose voice is con - tent- ment, whose pres - ence is balm:

Be there at our wak - ing, and give us, we pray,
Be there at our la - bors, and give us, we pray,
Be there at our hom - ing, and give us, we pray,
Be there at our sleep - ing, and give us, we pray,

Your bliss in our hearts, Lord, at the break of the day.
Your strength in our hearts, Lord, at the noon of the day.
Your love in our hearts, Lord, at the eve of the day.
Your peace in our hearts, Lord, at the end of the day.

This 20th-century text draws from events in Jesus' earthly life to
remind us that God's providence never fails throughout the day.

Text: Jan Struther, 1901–53
Tune: Irish folk; setting: Carlton R. Young, b. 1926

SLANE
10 11 11 12

Text: Oxford University Press
Tune: Public domain   Setting: © 1964 Abingdon Press, admin. The Copyright Company

Ps. 55:16–17

887   Go, My Children, with My Blessing

1 Go, My chil-dren, with My bless-ing, Nev - er a - lone.
2 Go, My chil-dren, sins for - giv - en, At peace and pure.
3 Go, My chil-dren, fed and nour-ished, Clo - ser to Me;
4 I the Lord will bless and keep you And give you peace;

Wak - ing, sleep-ing, I am with you; You are My own.
Here you learned how much I love you, What I can cure.
Grow in love and love by serv - ing, Joy - ful and free.
I the Lord will smile up - on you And give you peace:

In My love's bap - tis - mal riv - er I have made you Mine for - ev - er.
Here you heard My dear Son's sto - ry; Here you touched Him, saw His glo - ry.
Here My Spir - it's pow - er filled you; Here His ten - der com-fort stilled you.
I the Lord will be your Fa - ther, Sav - ior, Com - fort-er, and Broth-er.

Go, My chil-dren, with My bless-ing— You are My own.
Go, My chil-dren, sins for - giv - en, At peace and pure.
Go, My chil-dren, fed and nour-ished, Joy - ful and free.
Go, My chil-dren; I will keep you And give you peace.

*In this hymn, noted Lutheran hymnwriter Jaroslav Vajda crafts a blessing
that is spoken to us by the triune God. With His blessing we are at peace.*

Text: Jaroslav J. Vajda, b. 1919
Tune: Welsh melody, 18th century; setting: Ralph Vaughan Williams, 1872–1958

AR HYD Y NOS
84 84 88 84

Matt. 28: 20b; John 20:19–23; Num. 6:22–27; Eph. 5:25–33 (wedding stanza)

For use at weddings, the following stanza may be sung in place of stanzas 2 and 3:

In this union I have joined you husband and wife
Now, my children, live together as heirs of life:
Each the other's gladness sharing; Each the other's burdens bearing,
Now, my children, live together as heirs of life.

Children of the Heavenly Father 888

1 Chil - dren of the heav'n - ly Fa - ther Safe - ly
2 God His own doth tend and nour - ish; In His
3 Nei - ther life nor death shall ev - er From the
4 Though He giv - eth or He tak - eth, God His

in His bos - om gath - er; Nest - ling bird nor star in
ho - ly courts they flour - ish. From all e - vil things He
Lord His chil - dren sev - er; Un - to them His grace He
chil - dren ne'er for - sak - eth; His the lov - ing pur - pose

heav - en Such a ref - uge e'er was giv - en.
spares them; In His might - y arms He bears them.
show - eth, And their sor - rows all He know - eth.
sole - ly To pre - serve them pure and ho - ly.

*Children of the heavenly Father have always faced much adversity and loss.
Yet one thing remains constant—God's promise that He will not forsake us.*

Text: Caroline V. Sandell Berg, 1832–1903, tr. Ernest W. Olson, 1870–1958
Music: Swedish folk tune, *Lofsånger och andeliga wisor,* 1873

TRYGGARE KAN INGEN VARA
88 88 (Trochaic)

Rom. 8:14–17, 35–39; Matt. 6:26–27

889

There Is a Balm in Gilead

Refrain

There is a balm in Gil-e-ad to make the wound-ed whole;

There is a balm in Gil-e-ad to heal the sin - sick soul.

1 Some - times I feel dis - cour-aged and— think my work's in vain,
2 If you can - not preach like Pe - ter, if you can - not pray like Paul,
3 Don't— ev - er feel dis - cour-aged, for— Je - sus is your friend;

Refrain

But— then the Ho - ly Spir - it re - vives my soul a - gain.
You can tell the love of Je - sus and say, "He died for all."
And— if you lack for knowl-edge, He'll ne'er re - fuse to lend.

*Gilead was an ancient source of medicinal herbs. This African American
spiritual tells about the work of the Holy Spirit who points us to Jesus, the
Salve of healing for all lives bruised by sin.*

Text: African American spiritual
Music: African American spiritual

BALM IN GILEAD
Irregular

Text and music: Public domain

Jer. 8:18–9:2; 1 Peter 4:10–14

When Aimless Violence Takes Those We Love

1 When aim-less vi-o-lence takes those we love,
2 When pass-ing years rob sight and strength and mind
3 Our faith may flick-er low, and hope grow dim,
4 Be-cause Your Son knew ag-o-ny and loss,
5 Through long grief-dark-ened days help us, dear Lord,

When ran-dom death strikes child-hood's prom-ise down,
Yet fail to still a strong-ly beat-ing heart,
Yet You, O God, are with us in our pain;
Felt des-o-la-tion, grief and scorn and shame,
To trust Your grace for cour-age to en-dure,

When wrench-ing loss be-comes our dai-ly bread,
And grief be-comes the fab-ric of our days,
You grieve with us and for us day by day,
We know You will be with us, come what may,
To rest our souls in Your sup-port-ing love,

We know, O God, You leave us not a-lone.
Dear Lord, You do not stand from us a-part.
And with us, shar-ing sor-row, will re-main.
Your lov-ing pres-ence near, al-ways the same.
And find our hope with-in Your mer-cy sure.

Focusing on both random violence, one of the many ills plaguing modern
society, and other times of loss, this hymn seeks to point the grieving
individual to the steadfast mercy and all-sufficient grace of God.

Text: Joy F. Patterson, b. 1931
Tune: Alfred M. Smith, 1879–1971; setting: Richard W. Hillert, b. 1923

Text: © 1994, 1997 Hope Publishing Co.
Tune: © 1990 Church of the Ascension, Atlantic City, N.J.   Setting: © 1969 Concordia Publishing House

SURSUM CORDA
10 10 10 10

1 Peter 2:21–24; 4:12–14; 19

891 O Lord, Hear My Prayer

O Lord, hear my prayer. O Lord, hear my prayer,

when I call an - swer me. O Lord, hear my prayer. O

Lord, hear my prayer. Come and lis-ten to me. O me.

Text: Taizé Community, 1982
Music: Jacques Berthier, 1923–94

HEAR MY PRAYER
55 6 D

Text and music: © 1982, 1984 Les Presses de Taizé, admin. GIA Publications, Inc.

Ps. 31:2; 102:1–2

892 Come, Lord Jesus, Be Our Guest

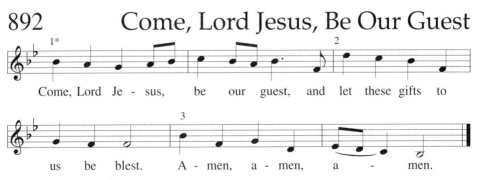

Come, Lord Je - sus, be our guest, and let these gifts to

us be blest. A - men, a - men, a - men.

* May be sung as a two- or three-part canon.

Text: German traditional
Tune: German traditional

KOMM, HERR JESU
PM

Text and tune: Public domain

Ps. 145:15–16; Luke 24:29–30; James 1:17a

Praise, My Soul, the King of Heaven 893

1 Praise, my soul, the King of hea - ven; To His feet your
2 Praise Him for His grace and fa - vor To His peo - ple
3 Fa - ther - like He tends and spares us; Well our fee - ble
4 An - gels, help us to a - dore Him; You be - hold Him

trib - ute bring; Ran - somed, healed, re - stored, for - giv - en,
in dis - tress; Praise Him still the same as ev - er,
frame He knows; In His hand He gen - tly bears us,
face to face; Sun and moon, bow down be - fore Him,

Ev - er - more His prais - es sing; Al - le - lu - ia,
Slow to chide, and swift to bless; Al - le - lu - ia,
Res - cues us from all our foes. Al - le - lu - ia,
All who dwell in time and space. Al - le - lu - ia,

al - le - lu - ia! Praise the ev - er - last - ing King.
al - le - lu - ia! Glo - rious in His faith - ful - ness.
al - le - lu - ia! Wide - ly yet His mer - cy flows.
al - le - lu - ia! Praise with us the God of grace.

Text: Henry F. Lyte, 1793–1874, alt.
Music: John Goss, 1800–80

LAUDA ANIMA (PRAISE, MY SOUL)
87 87 87

Ps. 103

894

Adoramus Te Domine

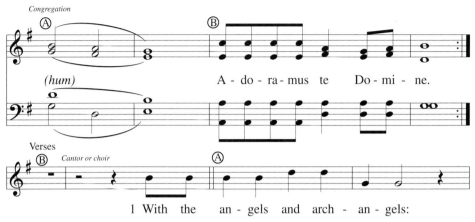

Congregation

(hum)

A - do - ra - mus te Do - mi - ne.

Verses

Cantor or choir

1 With the an - gels and arch - an - gels:

2 With the pa - tri - archs and proph - ets:

3 With the Vir - gin Mar - y, moth - er of God:

4 With the a - pos - tles and e - van - gel - ists:

5 With all the mar - tyrs of Christ:

6 With all who wit - ness to the Gos - pel of the Lord:

7 With all Your peo - ple of the Church through - out the world:

Adoramus te Domine (ah-doh-RAH-moos tay DOH-mee-nay): We adore You, Lord.

Text: Taizé Community, 1978
Music: Jacques Berthier, 1923–94

ADORAMUS TE
Irregular

Text and music: © 1978 Les Presses de Taizé, admin. GIA Publications, Inc.

Rev. 11:16–19

Voices Raised to You

895

1 Voic - es raised to You we of - fer; Tune them, God, for
2 All cre - a - tion joins to praise You; Earth and sky Your
3 Christ, the song of Love in - car - nate, Touch-ing earth with
4 Spir - it, flam - ing through cre - a - tion, Kin - dle faith with -
5 How can an - y praise we of - fer Mea - sure all the

songs of praise. Hearts and hands we bring in trib - ute
works dis - play. Art and mu - sic, gifts You lend us,
heav - en's grace, For Your liv - ing, suf - f'ring, dy - ing,
in each heart. Lift our voic - es high in cho - rus;
thanks we owe? Take our hearts and hands and voic - es—

For Your gifts through all our days. Al - le - lu - ia!
We re - turn to You to - day. Al - le - lu - ia!
For Your ris - ing, hear our praise! Al - le - lu - ia!
Through our hands Your love im - part. Al - le - lu - ia!
Gifts of love we can be - stow. Al - le - lu - ia!

Al - le - lu - ia! Tri - une God, to You we sing!
Al - le - lu - ia! God, Cre - a - tor, source of life!
Al - le - lu - ia! Christ, Re - deem - er, Lord of life!
Al - le - lu - ia! Spir - it, Help - er, breath of life!
Al - le - lu - ia! Tri - une God, to You we sing!

This hymn, written for the 10th anniversary of the Association of Lutheran Church
Musicians, calls us to use all of the creative gifts God has given us.

Text: Herman G. Stuempfle, Jr., b. 1923
Music: Carolyn Jennings, b. 1936

Text: © 1996 GIA Publications, Inc.
Music: © 1996 Carolyn Jennings

SONG OF PRAISE
87 87 87

Col. 3:16; Is. 12:2; 2 Cor. 4:13; Ps. 147:1

896

Alabaré

Refrain/Estribillo

A-la-ba - ré   a-la-ba - ré   a - la - ba-

ré   a mi Se - ñor.   A-la-ba - ré   a-la-ba-

ré   a - la - ba- ré a mi Se - ñor.

1 John saw the num - ber of all those re - deemed, And
1 *Juan vio el nú - me - ro de los re - di - mi-dos,* Y
2 Wor - thy is Christ— the Lamb who was slain, Whose
3 Sing with the peo - ple, the peo - ple of God, And

Alabaré a mi Señor (Ah-lah-bah-RAY ah mee Sen-YOR): I will praise my Lord.

The apostle John saw a vision of the redeemed praising the Lamb whose blood had cleansed them from all sin. We join our song with those who have gone before us and those in our own day "from every nation, tribe, people and language."

Text: Manuel José Alonso and José Pagán; English text: composite
Music: Manuel José Alonso and José Pagán

ALABARÉ
Irregular

Spanish text and music: © 1979 Manuel José Alonso, José Pagán, and Ediciones Musical PAX, admin. OCP Publications.
English text (sts. *2–*3): © 1998 Augsburg Fortress   English text (sts. 2–3): Public domain   *Rev. 5:8–13; 7:9–15*

all were sing - ing prais - es to the Lord.
to - dos a - la - ba - ban al Se - ñor:
blood has set us free from ev - 'ry sin.
join cre - a - tion in a joy - ful hymn.

Thou - sands were pray - ing, Ten thou - sands re - joic - ing, And
U - nos o - ra - ban, o - tros can - ta - ban, Mas
Pow - er and rich - es, And wis - dom and strength___ And
Bless - ing and hon - or And glo - ry and might___ To

Refrain/Estribillo

all were sing - ing prais - es to the Lord.
to - dos a - la - ba - ban al Se - ñor.
hon - or and all bless - ing shall be His.
God and to the Lamb be with - out end.

*2 Voices united in joy and in singing,
We offer praise and glory to our God:
To God the Father, to Christ the Savior,
And to the Holy Spirit, three in One.
Refrain

*3 We are Your people, O God everlasting,
The people You created out of love.
Mercy and justice, power and wisdom:
We bless You, we adore You without end.
Refrain

2 *Todos unidos, alegres cantemos
Gloria y alabanzas al Señor:
Gloria al Padre, gloria al Hijo,
Y gloria al Espíritu de amor.*
Estribillo

3 *Somos tu pueblo, Dios Padre eterno;
Tú nos has creado po amor.
Te adoramos, te bendecimos,
Y todos cantamos en tu honor.*
Estribillo

Stanzas 2 and 3 within the music are not a translation of the original Spanish, but a versification of Revelation 5 and 7.
*Stanzas *2 and *3 are a translation and may be sung in addition to or in place of stanzas 2 and 3 within the music.*

897 New Songs of Celebration Render

1 New songs of cel - e - bra - tion ren - der To Him who has great
2 Joy - ful - ly, heart - i - ly re - sound-ing, Let ev - 'ry in - stru -
3 Ri - vers and seas and tor - rents roar - ing, Hon - or the Lord with
4 Peo - ple from ev - 'ry tribe and na - tion, U - nite your songs with

won - ders done; Love sits en - throned in age - less
ment and voice Peal out the praise of grace a -
wild ac - claim; Moun - tains and stones, look up a -
that re - frain End - less - ly sung in ex - ul -

splen - dor; Come and a - dore the might - y One.
bound - ing, Call - ing the whole world to re - joice.
dor - ing, And find a voice to praise His name.
ta - tion: "Wor - thy is Christ, the Lamb once slain!"

He has made known His great sal - va - tion Which
Trum - pets and or - gans, set in mo - tion Such
Righ - teous, com - mand - ing, ev - er glo - rious, Prais -
Join all the crea - tures, high and low - ly, That

Text: Erik Routley, 1917–82, sts. 1–3; Stephen P. Starke, b. 1955, st. 4
Tune: att. Louis Bourgeois, c. 1510–61; setting: composite

RENDEZ À DIEU
98 98 D

Text: (sts.1–3): © 1974 Hope Publishing Co. Text (st. 4): © 1998 Hope Publishing Company
Tune: Public domain   Setting: © 1998 Hope Publishing Company

Psalm 98

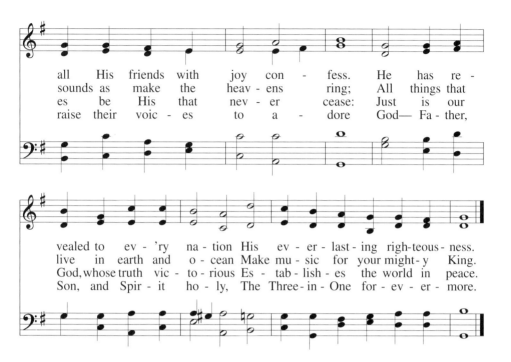

all His friends with joy con - fess. He has re -
sounds as make the heav - ens ring; All things that
es be His that nev - er cease: Just is our
raise their voic - es to a - dore God— Fa - ther,

vealed to ev - 'ry na - tion His ev - er - last - ing righ-teous - ness.
live in earth and o - cean Make mu - sic for your might- y King.
God, whose truth vic - to - rious Es - tab - lish - es the world in peace.
Son, and Spir - it ho - ly, The Three - in - One for - ev - er - more.

Father, We Thank Thee 898

1 Father, we thank Thee who hast planted
    Thy holy Name within our hearts.
Knowledge and faith and life immortal
    Jesus, Thy Son, to us imparts.
Thou, Lord, didst make all for Thy pleasure,
    Didst give us food for all our days,
Giving in Christ the Bread eternal;
    Thine is the pow'r, be Thine the praise.

2 Watch o'er Thy Church, O Lord, in mercy,
    Save it from evil, guard it still,
Perfect it in Thy love, unite it,
    Cleansed and conformed unto Thy will.
As grain, once scattered on the hillsides,
    Was in this broken bread made one,
So from all lands Thy Church be gathered
    Into Thy kingdom by Thy Son.

This hymn is to be sung to RENDEZ À DIEU.

Text: *Didache,* 2d century; tr. F. Bland Tucker, 1895–1984

John 6:22–58; 1 Cor. 10:16–17

899 Great Is Thy Faithfulness

1 Great is Thy faith - ful-ness, O God my Fa - ther;
2 Sum - mer and win - ter and spring-time and har - vest,
3 Par - don for sin and a peace that en - dur - eth,

There is no shad - ow of turn - ing with Thee;
Sun, moon, and stars in their cours - es a - bove
Thine own dear pres - ence to cheer and to guide;

Thou chang-est not, Thy com - pas - sions, they fail not;
Join with all na - ture in man - i - fold wit - ness
Strength for to - day and bright hope for to - mor - row,

As Thou hast been, Thou for - ev - er wilt be.
To Thy great faith - ful - ness, mer - cy, and love.
Bless-ings all mine, with ten thou - sand be - side!

*This hymn expresses the faith and conviction of the inspired prophet
Jeremiah: Even when things are dark and troubled, God's faithfulness
and mercy never fail. His grace and loving care do not change.*

Text: Thomas O. Chisholm, 1866–1960
Music: William M. Runyan, 1870–1957

FAITHFULNESS
11 10 11 10 and refrain

Lam. 3:22–24; James 1:17; Gen. 8:20–22; Ps. 89:1–2

900

Oh, Sing to the Lord

Text: Brazilian folk song; Spanish and English tr. Gerhard Cartford, b. 1923
Tune: Brazilian folk tune; setting: Gerhard Cartford, b. 1923

Text: © Gerhard Cartford
Tune: Public domain   Setting: © Gerhard Cartford

CANTAD AL SEÑOR
56 56 56 55

Psalm 98; 150; 1 Cor. 12:3

3 So dance for our God
   And blow all the trumpets.
So dance for our God
   And blow all the trumpets.
So dance for our God
   And blow all the trumpets,
And sing to our God,
   And sing to our God.

4 Oh, shout to our God,
   Who gave us the Spirit
Oh, shout to our God,
   Who gave us the Spirit
Oh, shout to our God,
   Who gave us the Spirit.
Oh, sing to our God,
   Oh, sing to our God.

5 For Jesus is Lord!
   Amen! Alleluia!
For Jesus is Lord!
   Amen! Alleluia!
For Jesus is Lord!
   Amen! Alleluia!
Oh, sing to our God,
   Oh, sing to our God.

3 *Cantad al Señor,*
   Alabadle con arpa.
Cantad al Señor
   Alabadle con arpa,
Cantad al Señor
   Alabadle con arpa,
¡Cantad al Señor,
   Cantad al Señor!

4 *Es él que nos da*
   El Espíritu Santo.
Es él que nos da
   El Espíritu Santo,
Es él que nos da
   El Espíritu Santo,
¡Cantad al Señor,
   Cantad al Señor!

5 *¡Jesús es Señor!*
   ¡Amén, aleluya!
¡Jesús es Señor!
   ¡Amén, aleluya!
¡Jesús es Señor!
   ¡Amén, aleluya!
¡Cantad al Señor,
   Cantad al Señor!

Now That the Daylight Fills the Sky

1 Now that the day - light fills the sky, We
2 Would guard our hearts and tongues from strife; From
3 So we, when this new day is gone, And
4 "All praise to You, cre - a - tor Lord! All

lift our hearts to God on high, That
an - ger's din would shield our life; From
night in turn is draw - ing on, With
praise to You, e - ter - nal Word! All

He, in all we do or say, Would
e - vil sights would turn our eyes, And
con - science by the world un - stained Shall
praise to You, O Spir - it wise!" We

keep us free from harm to - day;
close our ears to van - i - ties;
praise His name for vic - t'ry gained.
sing as day - light fills the skies.

This hymn may be sung in canon: the second voice entering
two beats after the first, as noted in the tenor line.

Text: Latin hymn, 7th or 8th cent.; tr. John M. Neale, 1818–66, alt.
Music: Dale Wood, b. 1934

LAUREL
LM

Ps. 4:1–3; 143:8–10; Phil. 4:7

Greet the Rising Sun

902

1 Greet the ris-ing sun, Shin-ing with bright force,
2 Fa-ther, hear my prayer, Keep me safe to-day;
3 Lord, I will to-day On Your love re-ly;

Like an ath-lete strong, Set to run the course;
Sanc-ti-fy my thoughts, All I do and say:
Let no e-vil thought Cloud the clear blue sky.

Birds soar high a-bove, Wild-flow'rs bloom be-low;
As I teach the young And es-teem the old,
Joy-ful and con-tent With life's sim-pler things,

With the day's new light, Glad to work I go.
May Your boun-teous grace By my life be told.
Know-ing all I need From Your kind-ness springs.

This morning hymn by a notable Chinese Christian theologian and leader,
Chao Tzu-chèn, is united with this Chinese folk tune and conveys the
believer's trust in God and prayerful anticipation of a new day of His grace.

Text: Chao Tzu-chèn, 1888–1979; English ver.: Stephen P. Starke, b. 1955
Tune: Chinese folk tune; setting: John Eggert, b. 1946

LE P'ING
55 55 55 55

Ps. 19:1–5; 32:10; 50:1–2; Col. 3:17; Matt. 6:26, 28

903

Christ, Mighty Savior

1 Christ, might - y Sav - ior, Light of all cre - a - tion,
2 Now comes the day's end as the sun is set - ting:
3 There - fore we come now eve - ning rites to of - fer,
4 Give heed, we pray You, to our sup - pli - ca - tion:
5 Though bod - ies slum - ber, hearts shall keep their vig - il,

You make the day - time ra - diant with the sun - light
Mir - ror of day - break, pledge of res - ur - rec - tion;
Joy - ful - ly chant - ing ho - ly hymns to praise You,
That You may grant us par - don for of - fens - es,
For - ev - er rest - ing in the peace of Je - sus,

With vivid images, this ancient text not only paints a picture of the beauty of evening but also encourages prayer and praise—faith's response to God at day's end. Both of these textual aspects are reinforced by this wonderfully expressive tune.

Text: Mozarabic, 10th cent.; tr. Alan McDougall, 1895–1964 and Anne LeCroy, b. 1930
Music: Richard W. Dirksen, b. 1921

INNISFREE FARM
11 11 11 5

John 1:1–5; Psalm 4; 134; Heb. 4:8–10

And   to   the night give   glit - ter - ing   a - dorn - ment,
While   in   the heav - ens   choirs of stars ap - pear - ing
With   all   cre - a - tion   join - ing hearts and voic - es,
Strength for   our weak hearts,   rest for ach - ing bod - ies,
In   light or   dark - ness   wor - ship - ing our Sav - ior

Stars   in   the   heav   -   ens.
Hal   -   low   the   night   -   fall.
Sing   -   ing   Your   glo   -   ry.
Sooth -   ing   the   wea   -   ry.
Now   and   for - ev   -   er.

904

The Day Thou Gavest

1 The day Thou gav - est, Lord, is end - ed,
2 We thank Thee that Thy Church, un - sleep - ing
3 As o'er each con - ti - nent and is - land
4 The sun, that bids us rest, is wak - ing
5 So be it, Lord! Thy throne shall nev - er,

The dark - ness falls at Thy be - hest;
While earth rolls on - ward in - to light,
The dawn leads on an - oth - er day,
Thy chil - dren un - der west - ern skies,
Like earth's proud em - pires, pass a - way;

To Thee our morn - ing hymns as - cend - ed,
Through all the world her watch is keep - ing,
The voice of prayer is nev - er si - lent,
And hour by hour, as day is break - ing,
Thy king - dom stands and grows for - ev - er,

Thy praise shall hal - low now our rest.
And nev - er rests by day or night.
Nor dies the strain of praise a - way.
Fresh hymns of thank - ful praise a - rise.
Till all Thy crea - tures own Thy sway.

Text: John Ellerton, 1826–93, alt.
Music: Clement C. Scholefield, 1839–1904

Text and music: Public domain

ST. CLEMENT
98 98

Rom. 13:11–12; Ps. 113:2–4

For the Fruits of His Creation

905

1 For the fruits of His cre - a - tion, Thanks be to God.
2 In the just re - ward of la - bor, God's will is done.
3 For the har - vests of the Spir - it, Thanks be to God.

For His gifts to ev - 'ry na - tion, Thanks be to God.
In the help we give our neigh - bor, God's will is done.
For the good we all in - her - it, Thanks be to God.

For the plow - ing, sow - ing, reap - ing, Si - lent growth while we are sleep - ing,
In our world - wide task of car - ing For the hun - gry and de - spair - ing,
For the won - ders that as - tound us, For the truths that still con - found us,

Fu - ture needs in earth's safe - keep - ing, Thanks be to God.
In the har - vests we are shar - ing, God's will is done.
Most of all, that love has found us, Thanks be to God.

Text: Fred Pratt Green, b. 1903
Music: Welsh melody, 18th century; setting: Ralph Vaughan Williams, 1872–1958

Text: © 1984 Hope Publishing Co.
Music: Public domain

AR HYD Y NOS
84 84 88 84

Mark 4:26–27; 2 Cor. 9:6–12, 15

906   Eternal Father, Strong to Save

1 E - ter - nal Fa - ther, strong to save, Whose arm hath bound the
2 O Christ, the Lord of hill and plain O'er which our traf - fic
3 O Spir - it, whom the Fa - ther sent To spread a - broad the
4 O Trin - i - ty of love and pow'r, Our peo - ple shield in

rest - less wave, Who bidd'st the might - y o - cean deep Its
runs a - main By moun - tain pass or val - ley low; Wher -
firm - a - ment; O Wind of heav - en, by Thy might Save
dan - ger's hour; From rock and tem - pest, fire and foe, Pro -

own ap - point - ed lim - its keep: Oh, hear us when we
ev - er, Lord, Thy peo - ple go, Pro - tect them by Thy
all who dare the ea - gle's flight, And keep them by Thy
tect them where - so - e'er they go; Thus ev - er - more shall

cry to Thee For those in per - il on the sea.
guard - ing hand From ev - 'ry per - il on the land.
watch - ful care From ev - 'ry per - il in the air.
rise to Thee Glad praise from air and land and sea.

More than ever we are people on the go, often unaware of the miracle of travel. As
we were baptized into the name of the triune God, so we begin our day, work, and
travel under His gracious care.

Text: William Whiting, 1825–78, sts. 1, *2, *3, 4, alt.; Robert N. Spencer, 1877–1961, sts. 2–3, alt.
Music: John Bacchus Dykes, 1823–76

MELITA
88 88 88

Mark 4:35–41; Gen. 1:1–8; Psalm 3

The following stanzas from the original Navy Hymn may be substituted:

*2 O Christ, whose voice the waters heard
   And hushed their raging at Thy word,
   Who walkedst on the foaming deep,
   And calm amid its rage didst sleep:
   O hear us when we cry to Thee,
   For those in peril on the sea.

*3 Most Holy Spirit, who didst brood
   Upon the chaos dark and rude,
   And bid its angry tumult cease,
   And give, for wild confusion, peace:
   O hear us when we cry to Thee,
   For those in peril on the sea.

CANTICLES AND SERVICE MUSIC

Alleluia

907

Text: Traditional
Music: Jacques Berthier, 1923–94

Music: © 1984 Les Presses de Taizé, admin. GIA Publications, Inc.
Text: Public domain

ALLELUIA
Irregular

908 Sing Praise to the God of Israel

1 Sing praise to the God of Is - ra - el! Sing praise for His
2 God spoke by the proph - ets long a - go, His prom - ise on
3 You, child, will go on be - fore the Lord As proph - et, His
4 O bright, ris - ing Sun now shine on us In need of il -

vis - i - ta - tion! Re - deem - ing His peo - ple from their
oath re - call - ing— To A - bra - ham made in for - mer
way pre - par - ing; To speak on be - half of God Most
lu - mi - na - tion; Come scat - ter the shades of sin and

sin, Ac - com - plish - ing their sal - va - tion, Up - rais - ing a
years: Of van - quish - ing foes ap - pall - ing, That those He de -
High, His coun - sel of truth de - clar - ing: Rich mer - cy and
death And shat - ter their dom - i - na - tion. Be guid - ing our

might - y horn with - in The house of His ser - vant Da - vid!
liv - ered from their fears Might glad - ly and tru - ly serve Him.
grace for all where - by In - iq - ui - ty is for - giv - en.
foot - steps on the path Of peace, in Your pres - ence dawn - ing!

This text is a versification of the Benedictus, Zechariah's song of
praise to God at the birth of his son, John (the Baptist). The unusual
rhyme scheme (abcbcd) is set off by this 19th century Danish folk tune.

Text: Stephen P. Starke, b. 1955
Music: Christoph Weyse, 1774–1842

Text: Copyright © 1992 Stephen P. Starke
Music: Public domain

DEN SIGNEDE DAG
98 98 98

Luke 1:68–79

Tell Out, My Soul, the Greatness of the Lord

1 Tell out, my soul, the great-ness of the Lord!
2 Tell out, my soul, the great-ness of His name!
3 Tell out, my soul, the great-ness of His might!
4 Tell out, my soul, the glo-ries of His Word!

Un - num - bered bless-ings give my spir-it voice;
Make known His might, the deeds His arm has done;
Pow'rs and do - min-ions lay their glo-ry by.
Firm is His prom-ise, and His mer-cy sure.

Ten - der to me the prom-ise of His Word;
His mer - cy sure, from age to age the same;
Proud hearts and stub - born wills are put to flight,
Tell out, my soul, the great-ness of the Lord

In God my Sav - ior shall my heart re - joice.
His ho - ly name— the Lord, the Might - y One.
The hun - gry fed, the hum - ble lift - ed high.
To chil - dren's chil - dren and for ev - er - more!

This paraphrase of the Magnificat is based on the New English Bible *translation.*

Text: Timothy Dudley-Smith, b. 1926
Music: Walter Greatorex, 1877–1949

WOODLANDS
10 10 10 10

Luke 1:46–55

910 Splendor and Honor

1 Splen-dor and hon - or, maj - es - ty and pow - er,
2 Praised be the true Lamb, slain for our re - demp - tion,
3 To the Al - might - y, throned in heav-'nly splen - dor,

Are Yours, O Lord God, fount of ev - 'ry bless - ing,
By whose self - of - f'ring we are made God's peo - ple:
And to the Sav - ior, Christ our Lamb and Shep - herd,

For by Your bid - ding was the whole cre - a - tion
A priest-ly king - dom, from all tongues and na - tions,
Be ad - o - ra - tion, praise, and glo - ry giv - en,

Called in - to be - ing.
Called to God's ser - vice.
Now and for - ev - er.

*This versification of selected hymns of praise from the book of
Revelation is especially appropriate as a substitution for the
GLORIA IN EXCELSIS during the Great Fifty Days of Easter.*

Text: Carl P. Daw, Jr., b. 1944
Music: K. Lee Scott, b. 1950

Text: © 1990 Hope Publishing Co.
Music: © 1987 MorningStar Music Publishers

SHADES MOUNTAIN
11 11 11 5

Rev. 4:11; 5:9–10, 13; 7:9–17

Lord, Bid Your Servant Go in Peace 911

1 Lord, bid Your ser - vant go in peace, Your
2 This is the Sav - ior of the world, The

word is now ful - filled. These eyes have seen sal -
Gen - tiles' prom - ised light, God's glo - ry dwell - ing

va - tion's dawn, This child so long fore - told.
in our midst, The joy of Is - ra - el.

Text: James Quinn, b. 1919
Music: American folk tune; setting: Henry V. Gerike, b. 1948

Text: © 1969 James Quinn, admin. Selah Music
Tune: Public domain   Setting: © 1998 Concordia Publishing House

LAND OF REST
CM

Luke 2:29–32

912 Jesus Sat with His Disciples

Text: Stephen P. Starke, b. 1955
Music: Marty Haugen, b. 1950

Text: © 1997 Stephen P. Starke
Music: © 1987 GIA Publications, Inc.

JOYOUS LIGHT
87 87 D

Matt. 5:1–12; Luke 6:20–26

king - dom they will share. Bless-ed are the sad and
will to them be shown. And the pure in heart are
king - dom up a - bove— So be glad to share My

mourn - ing, Joy and com-fort will be theirs.
bless - ed, They have eyes for God a - lone.
suf - f'ring And re - joice to know My love."

Kyrie

913

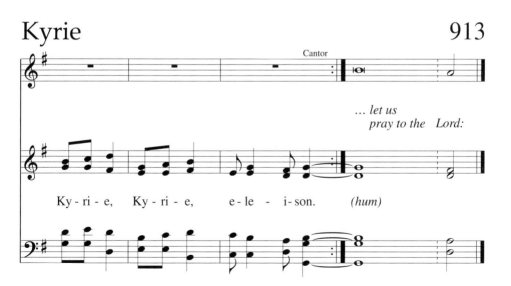

Cantor

... let us
pray to the Lord:

Ky - ri - e, Ky - ri - e, e - le - i - son. (hum)

Kyrie eleison (KIR-ee-ay ay-LAY-ee-sohn): Lord, have mercy.

Text: Traditional
Music: Jacques Berthier, 1923–94

Text: Public domain
Music: © 1981 Les Presses de Taizé, admin. GIA Publications, Inc.

KYRIE
Irregular

Mark 10:47

All You Works of God, Bless the Lord!

914

1 All you works of God, bless the Lord!
2 Sing, you sun and you moon a - bove,
3 Frost of win - ter with song so cold,
4 Hills and moun - tains, now sing His worth,

All you an - gels, now bless the Lord;
Stars of heav - en, now sing His love;
Dews of sum - mer, your song un - fold;
All you green things that grow on earth;

Come you heav - ens and pow'rs that be,
Dew and show - ers, you winds that blow,
Light and dark - ness, you day and night,
Seas and riv - ers, you springs and wells,

Praise the Lord and His maj - es - ty:
Heat and fire, you ice and snow:
Clouds of thun - der, you light - nings bright:
Beasts and cat - tle, you birds and whales:

Shadrach, Meshach, and Abednego praised God as they stood in the fiery furnace (the Apocryphal "Song of the Three Young Men"). The Jamaican folk tune carries us along with all of God's works in praise of His majesty.

Text: Stephen P. Starke, b. 1955
Music: Jamaican folk tune; adapt. Doreen Potter, 1925–80

LINSTEAD
88 88 and refrain

Song of the Three Young Men; Ps. 103:20–22

Refrain

Raise your voic - es high, praise and mag - ni - fy,

All you works of God, bless the Lord!

Raise your voic - es high, praise and mag - ni - fy,

All you works of God, bless the Lord!

5 Come humanity, sing along,
Sing, you people of God, a song;
Priests and servants, your Lord now bless,
Join, you spirits and souls at rest.

Refrain

6 Bless the Lord, all you pure of heart;
All you humble, His praises start;
God the Father and Son adore,
Bless the Spirit forevermore!

Refrain

ACKNOWLEDGMENTS

Other than the copyrights listed below, the liturgical material on pages 6–46 is covered by the copyright of this book.

Liturgical responses and collects from *Lutheran Worship* © 1982 Concordia Publishing House.

Luther's Small Catechism © 1986 Concordia Publishing House.

Holy Bible, New International Version® © 1973, 1978, 1984 by International Bible Society. Used by permission of Zondervan Publishing House.

New King James Version © 1979, 1982. Used by permission.

Copyrighted material from the Divine Service, pages 6–16:

KYRIE — Text: public domain. Music: Healey Willan, 1880–1968 © 1959. Used by permission of the estate.

GLORIA IN EXCELSIS — Text: Edwin LeGrice, 1911–92 © 1991 Kevin Mayhew Ltd., License no. 799040. Music: Walter Greatorex, 1877–1949 © Oxford University Press.

GOSPEL ACCLAMATION — Text: public domain. Tune (refrain): Howard Hughes, b. 1930 © 1972, 1983 GIA Publications, Inc. Music (verse): composite © 1998 Concordia Publishing House.

SANCTUS — Text: Stephen P. Starke, b. 1955 © 1998 Concordia Publishing House. Music: Carl F. Schalk, b. 1929 © 1983 Augsburg Publishing House, admin. Augsburg Fortress.

AGNUS DEI — Text: Stephen P. Starke, b. 1955 © 1998 Concordia Publishing House. Music: public domain.

NUNC DIMITTIS — Text: Ernest Ryden, 1886–1981, st. 1 © Board of Publications, Lutheran Church in America, admin. Augsburg Fortress; Stephen P. Starke, b. 1955, st. 2 © 1998 Concordia Publishing House. Music: public domain.

Copyrighted material from Evening Prayer, pages 17–23:

HYMN OF LIGHT — Text: Carl P. Daw, Jr., b. 1944 © 1989 Hope Publishing Co. Music: public domain.

MAGNIFICAT — Text: Stephen P. Starke, b. 1955 © 1991 Stephen P. Starke. Music: public domain.

Composers of psalm tones and antiphons:

Mark Bangert, b. 1938 (Ps. 112) © 1978 *Lutheran Book of Worship.*

Henry V. Gerike, b. 1948 (Ps. 30, 40, 42, 47, 85, 97, 99) © 1998 Concordia Publishing House.

Paul J. Grime, b. 1958 (Psalm antiphons) © 1998 Concordia Publishing House.

Richard W. Hillert, b. 1923 (Ps. 31, 33, 141) © 1978 *Lutheran Book of Worship.*

Commission on Worship members: Mark Bender, Barbara Bradfield, Stephen Everette, Ronald Feuerhahn, Roger Pittelko, Richard Resch, Elizabeth Werner; Paul Grime, executive director.

Supplement Committee members: Ronald Feuerhahn, Henry Gerike, Paul Grime (project director), Joseph Herl, Timothy Quill, Richard Resch, Stephen Starke, Jon Vieker.

Concordia Publishing House staff: Henry Gerike (editor), Richard W. Gieseke, David A. Johnson, Mary Lou Kopp, John Krus, Don Petering, Anita Varney.

Other contributors: Mark Bender, Gertrude Conboy, Winnie Edwards, Ronald Feuerhahn, Kathleen Furman, Lynda Lorenz, Janet Muth, Larry Myers, Annette Schroeder.

COPYRIGHT HOLDERS AND ADMINISTRATORS

Abingdon Press
(*See* The Copyright Company)

Archdiocese of Philadelphia
Music Office
222 North 17th Street   Phone: 215-587-3696
Philadelphia, PA 19103-1299 Fax: 215-587-3561

Augsburg Fortress Publishers
P. O. Box 1209   Phone: 800-421-0239
Minneapolis, MN 55440-1209   Fax: 800-722-7766

Church Publishing, Inc.
(Church Pension Fund)   Phone: 212-592-1800
445 Fifth Avenue   or 800-223-6602
New York, NY 10016   Fax: 212-779-3392

Concordia Publishing House
Copyrights and Permissions
3558 S. Jefferson Avenue   Phone: 800-325-0191
St. Louis, MO 63118-3968   Fax: 314-268-1329

The Copyright Company
40 Music Square East   Phone: 615-244-5588
Nashville, TN 37203   Fax: 615-244-5591

CRC Publishing Company
2850 Kalamazoo Avenue, SE   Phone: 616-224-0785
Grand Rapids, MI 49560   Fax: 616-224-0834

GIA Publications
7404 South Mason Avenue   Phone: 800-442-1358
Chicago, IL 60638   Fax: 708-496-3828

The Ethiopian Evangelical Church MeKane Yesus
(Ye Etiopia Wongelawit Bete—Kristian MeKane Yesus)
P.O. Box 2087
Addis Ababa
ETHIOPIA

Hal Leonard Corporation
7777 West Bluemound Road
P.O. Box 13819   Phone: 414-774-3630
Milwaukee, WI 53213   Fax: 414-774-3259

Hope Publishing Company
380 South Main Place   Phone: 800-323-1049
Carol Stream, IL 60188   Fax: 630-665-2552

**International Committee on English
in the Liturgy (ICEL)**
1275 K Street, NW, Suite 1000
Washington, DC 20005   Phone: 202-347-0800

Kevin Mayhew, Ltd.
Rattlesden
Bury Street Edmunds,
Suffolk   Phone: 011-144-449-73-7978
ENGLAND 1P30 O8Z   Fax: 011-144-449-73-7834

Lutheran Theological College at Makumira
Tanzania, East Africa
c/o Concordia Publishing House

MorningStar Music Publishers
2117 59th Street   Phone: 800-647-2117
St. Louis, MO 63110   Fax: 314-647-2777

Novello and Company, Ltd.
8/9 Frith Street
London W1V 5TZ   Phone: 011-44-171-434-0066
ENGLAND   Fax: 011-44-171-287-6329

Oregon Catholic Press Publications
5536 NE Hassalo   Phone: 503-281-1191
Portland, OR 97213   Fax: 503-282-3486

Oxford University Press
Hymn Copyright
Great Clarendon Street
Oxford 0X26DP   Phone: 011-44-1865-556-767
ENGLА'   Fax: 011-44-1865-556-646

Oxford University Press
198 Madison Avenue   Phone: 800-334-4249 (x6048)
New York, NY 10016   Fax: 212-726-6444

Selah Publishing Company
58 Pearl Street
P.O. Box 3037   Phone: 914-338-2816
Kingston, NY 12401   Fax: 914-338-2991

The United Methodist Publishing House
(*See* The Copyright Company)

World Library Publications
3825 N. Willow Road   Phone: 800-621-5197
Schiller Park, IL 60176-0003 Fax: 847-671-5715

SCRIPTURAL INDEX

SCRIPTURAL INDEX

TOPICAL INDEX

TEXT AND MUSIC SOURCES

188

TUNES—METER

TITLES AND FIRST LINES